Saint Endellion

The Arms of
The Collegiate Church
of Saint Endelienta

SAINT ENDELLION

Essays on the Church, its Patron Saint and her Collegiate Foundation

EDWIN STARK, S.R.C., M.A.
Prebendary of Marnays in the
Collegiate Church of St Endellion

DYLLANSOW TRURAN

First published in 1983
Dyllansow Truran
Trewolsta, Trewirgie, Redruth, Cornwall

Dedicated to the late Thomas and Phoebe Stark, my parents, who first brought me to the vicinity of St Endelienta's Shrine and to Miss Margaret Sellon and Miss Elspeth Coe, my friends, who first welcomed me to it.

Printed and bound in Great Britain by
A. Wheaton & Co. Ltd, Exeter

ISBN 0–907566–62–6

Contents

Foreword

One of the last official acts which I performed before my translation to London was the collation of the Reverend Edwin Stark to the Prebend of Marnays in the Collegiate Church of St Endellion. I invited Father Stark to accept this appointment because I knew of the great devotion to St Endelienta and something of the work which he had already done both on her life and on the history of the Collegiate Church.

It was a great joy to me on my arrival in Cornwall in 1973 to learn that the rehabilitation of the College begun by Bishop Walter Frere had been sealed by a Pastoral Scheme early that year. But I also realized that if such an institution were to continue for posterity, mere schemes or statutes would in themselves prove insufficient. It must develop and continue a life of its own and its tradition must be a living one. I therefore tried to do my best to encourage this, beginning with my visit to the Chapter in 1974.

It is cause of just satisfaction to me that by publishing this Book of Essays Prebendary Stark should have made such a notable contribution to this process. What priests and laymen, men and women, who have visited this glorious Shrine, have known in their bones has in these essays been given solid foundation, on which devotion and love can be built in the future.

These essays are lucid, learned and judicious, both with regard to St Endelienta and her Church and to the history of Christianity in the Age of the Saints. I hope they will be read widely and encourage understanding of, and support for, this most beautiful and holy place.

May St Endelienta pray for us that true religion and sound learning may flourish through the worship of God in liturgy and music at her Shrine.

✠ GRAHAM LONDIN

Illustrations

Preface

At a Solemn Eucharist in the Church of St Endellion in the Deanery of Trigg Minor a ceremony of considerable interest and importance took place on 2nd May 1929. This ceremony, over which Dr Walter Frere, Lord Bishop of Truro presided, was the rehabilitation or reincorporation of the ancient Prebendal or Collegiate Church of St Endelienta. The Bishop, later that day, spoke about the foundation for the rehabilitation or reincorporation of which he was largely responsible. Canon Thomas Taylor, later that year, published an account of its constitution and history.

Some fifty years after these events would seem a not unsuitable time to commemorate them by offering some essays about St Endelienta and her foundation. Such a pleasant task presents problems which one must endeavour to take up from the point reached by previous writers. Among the latter I owe a special debt of gratitude to that triumvirate of authoritative scholars Canon Gilbert Doble, Canon Thomas Taylor and Mr Charles Henderson. Their painstaking and invaluable researches and their scholarly works have helped me, not least, in weighing up all the available evidence. I am also equally indebted to other scholars mentioned in footnotes and in the bibliography. To the best of my ability I have tried to distinguish carefully between subjective judgment (personal opinion) and objective matters of fact.

For the identity of St Endelienta there are numerous lists of the Children of Brychan though it might be said, if one may be permitted to borrow a phrase from the English epigrammatic writer C.C. Colton, that: "There is safety in numbers is the maxim of the foolish; there is ruin in numbers [is the maxim] of the wise." It is not unknown for hagiographers and historians to have been confused by the lists of the Children of Brychan concerning the identity of St Endelienta. W.C. Borlase in *The Age of the Saints* identifies her with St Teilo. Frances Arnold-Forster in her comprehensive *Studies in Church Dedications of England's Patron Saints* does likewise. W.S. Lach-

Szyrma in *A Church History of Cornwall and of the Diocese of Truro* goes even further. He would have us look at the list as given by W.C. Borlase and his comment concerning St Endelienta is certainly not one of unqualified praise: "St Endelient (a very dubious person), whose existence is questionable". Her existence and identity is, however, not doubtful, as I hope to demonstrate, and her biographer, Nicholas Roscarrock, will prove an excellent guide concerning the sort of person she was.

For the history of her foundation, sources come from the Episcopal Registers of the Diocese of Exeter (Institutions of Prebends and Visitations), various English historical documents, College Registers and local family histories. Unfortunately, Cornwall is not rich in Medieval Cartularies. Only those of four foundations spring to mind. The Regestrum Munimentorum (fifteenth century) of Launceston Priory is at Lambeth (MS 719) and there is a fourteenth to fifteenth century Formulary in the Bodleian Library (Tanner 196). There is a late fourteenth century General Cartulary of the Benedectine Priory on St Michael's Mount (Hatfield MS 315). The late W.S. Rashleigh had in his possession a Register (*c.* 1440) of Charters and other documents relating to the College of St Thomas, Glasney. There is a fragment of a late fifteenth century register relating to the Collegiate Church of St Buryan in the University Library at Cambridge (Ee. 5. 34).

Of such documentary evidence relating to St Endelienta's foundation there would seem to be no trace. The foundation is not mentioned in the original edition of Sir William Dugdale's *Monasticon Anglicanum*[1] produced from a vast collection of monastic charters and other documents relating to the history of English monasteries and collegiate churches. It is mentioned in John Tanner's *Notitia Monastica*[2] and this entry is copied in the revised edition of Dugdale's great work produced by J. Caley, R. Ellis and B. Blandinel.[3] J. Caley's copy of Tanner's *Notitia Monastica* has some MS notes in Caley's hand but these only refer to the *Valor Ecclesiasticus* and to Lyson's work on

[1] Issued in three volumes published in 1655, 1661 and 1673.

[2] Published 1744; reprinted 1787.

[3] Published 1817–30 (6 Vols.), 1846 (8 Vs.).

Cornwall. George Oliver's *Monasticon Dioecesis Exoniensis*[4] has a somewhat larger entry relating to St Endelienta's foundation. One is forced to the conclusion that any documents possessed by the foundation during the early period of its existence have been irretrievably lost. They were certainly not even recorded by Dugdale, Tanner and Oliver.

Sir John Maclean, in his comprehensive *Parochial and Family History of the Deanery of Trigg Minor,* reports that all Parish Registers at St Endellion earlier than 1732 were also lost and that those remaining at the time he wrote his great work (1873) were in a very bad condition.

Since the rehabilitation of St Endelienta's foundation, however, the Minutes Book of the Chapter is to hand and I am grateful to Canon Walter Prest (Rector and Prebendary of St Endellion 1970–81 and now Prebendary Emeritus) for his kindness in allowing me to refer to them. To him and his wife I am grateful for many kindnesses and much encouragement in the writing of these essays.

To the Lord Bishop of London, Dr Graham Leonard, who was Lord Bishop of Truro when I began writing these essays I am grateful not only for his interest in, and encouragement apropos, a pleasant task but also for his characteristic kindness in consenting to write a Foreword to these essays. This Foreword redeems their defects, makes them all the more worthwhile and will encourage people to read them.

The reproduciton of N. Roscarrock's biography of St Endelient (Ms Add.3041 ff.202v–203r upper half) is by permission of the Syndics of Cambridge University Library which I gratefully acknowledge. To the Royal Institution of Cornwall I am indebted for the sight of the late Charles Henderson's MS notes on St Endelienta. Would that that great scholar were alive to undertake what an amateur has nevertheless attempted.

EDWIN STARK
Feast of St Endelienta, 1982

[4] Published 1846.

The Collegiate Church of St Endelienta

In a delightful essay on St Endellion, Sir John Betjeman likens its parish church to a hare. "The ears," he says, "are the pinnacles of the tower and the rest of the hare, the church, crouches among wind-slashed firs."[1] Another comparison might be to liken the tower to a sentinel guarding the shrine of its Patron Saint.

This predominately fifteenth century building stands on a ridge of high ground and its tower, of three stages and built of great granite blocks said to have come from Lundy Island, is prominent on the skyline from land and sea. The approach to the church is along the B3314 road from Wadebridge to Delabole, to which road it lies adjacent. A short path leads to the south porch, splendidly wrought in granite and incorporating a sundial.

On entering the church, one is immediately aware of its well-lit spaciousness. The nave and chancel are low and wide and so are the aisles which extend to the east wall of the church. The light from the clear glass windows adds to the impression of space. Those of the aisles are of three lights and that of the east window of the chancel is of five lights.

The impression of spaciousness is accompanied by an awareness of the atmosphere of the church. The use of the word 'atmosphere' in its figurative sense refers to mental, spiritual and supernatural environment. To some, the atmosphere of the Collegiate Church of St Endelienta will be merely peaceful. To others, it will also be prayerful. Sir John Betjeman says of it: "Indeed, the church gives the impression that it goes on praying day and night whether there are people in it or not."[2] It is certainly a place in which prayer has been, and is, wont to be made. Yet others will be aware of a 'presence' within it. The Blessed Sacrament is reserved in an aumbry but, quite apart from this, is it possible that St Endelienta is, in some inexplicable way, present too? Such a possibility would

[1] *The Best of Betjeman*, p.147.

[2] *Collins Guide to English Parish Churches*, p.123.

seem to have crossed the mind of James Turner who relates that he and a friend were in the church late one summer night. He continues: "All the light we had was the moon through the clear glass windows and the hanging light before the Sacrament. Endelient could well have been there with us...."[3] The discernment of a 'presence' or of relics (the gift of 'hierognosis' which is a variant of what psychical researchers commonly call 'psychometry') are subjects beyond the scope of this essay. It suffices to say that the saints in Heaven may well watch over the scene of their labours on Earth.[4]

A suitable place at which to begin a study of the interior of the church is at the holy water stoup in the south wall immediately to the right of the south porch. This stoup is of great beauty and interest. It is of carved catacleuse stone, of superb craftsmanship and bears the coats of arms of three ancient Cornish families.

Catacleuse stone[5] came from a medieval quarry in the parish of St Merryn, near Padstow. In the late fourteenth century it commended itself to local craftsmen because, like Cornish granite, it was durable. Evidence of its use *c.* 1400, may be seen, for example, in the fonts at St Merryn and Padstow, the crosses at Mawgan and St Kew and the stoup and shrine at St Endellion. The production of these works of Cornish art in some local workshop is associated with the mysterious 'Master of Endellion' of whose life nothing is known. The traditional title accorded him is, however, of some significance.

Medieval masons may be separated into three groups. There were the 'rough-masons' who laid the stone which they had hewed. There were the 'free-masons' who worked on windows and doors and carved capitals. The greater their skill, the more elaborate the work they were able to undertake. There were the specialists who carved effigies and tombs, working in hard stone. Over these was the master-mason who, in addition to being a skilled craftsman himself, was probably responsible for providing plans, selecting suitable materials and engaging

[3] *The Stone Peninsula*, p.139.

[4] For 'hierognosis' see the study of Anne Catherine Emmerich in *Surprising Mystics*, by S.J. Herbert Thurston, p.68.

[5] Carrack-looze–grey-blue rock.

all employed in building construction over whom he supervised.

The significance of the title 'Master of Endellion' may well be that this mysterious figure, known to his local contemporaries who bequeathed his fame to posterity, was not only the sculptor of the stoup and the shrine in the Church of St Endelienta (*c.* 1400) but also the master-mason in charge of the building of that church, somewhat later during the fifteenth century, by a band of local craftsmen assisted, possibly, by itinerant crafsmen and, certainly, by local unskilled labourers. The composition of this work-force is of interest. It would need not only the three groups of masons mentioned above (all of which, in Cornwall, would have to work in hard stone–granite and catacleuse) but also carpenters, smiths, unskilled labourers and carters. It is difficult to say if any of those itinerant builders who journeyed through the land in the Middle Ages, adding to their experience and to the variety of their designs, were among this work-force. On the evidence of the decoration of the capitals of the pillars of the Church of St Endelienta (see p. 4), some craftsmen would certainly seem to have travelled from Devonshire.

Although the identity of the 'Master of Endellion' remains a mystery and we know nothing of his life, perhaps we may glean some information about him from the evidence of the work attributed to him and of that over which he had the supervision. On such evidence we might say that he was a devout man, a skilful craftsman and an excellent master-mason. This assessment is justified by his traditional title.[6]

The stoup is of interest, thirdly, because it incorporates the coats of arms of the Chenduit and Pentire families in the upper portion and those of the Roscarrock family in the lower portion. These three families intermarried. In the fourteenth century, John Roscarrock married Alice Chenduit and, in the fifteenth century, his great-grandson, John Roscarrock, mar-

[6] Biographies of medieval English architects and craftsmen are rare because of the obscurity of their lives. Only two medieval architects are included in the *Dictionary of National Biography*. Henry Yevele (*c.* 1320–1400) has a full-length biography–that by J.H. Harvey. Yevele, however, worked largely in London. Had the 'Master of Endellion' not worked in remote Cornwall only, he might well have achieved more than local fame.

ried Alice Pentire. The families were probably thus commemorated because they were benefactors of the parish, contributing to the cost of building the church.

Before turning our attention to the shrine of St Endelienta, situated in the south chapel, we shall consider the south aisle along which it is approached. We may as well consider the north aisle at the same time. It might be said of the aisles that they are almost identical architectural twins. They are of five bays, with arcades of Cornish standard granite design with four-centred arches. These (ogee) arches rest upon pillars, seen to full advantage since the lowering of the floor of the church to its original level (1937–8). Some of the capitals have the type of decoration (large horizontal leaves) standard in the churches of Devonshire. The aisles are wider than the seating which they contain. The bench ends, of English oak, were admirably fashioned by local craftsmen about forty years ago. They do not detract, in any way, from the ancient ones in the nave, which are of standard Perpendicular Cornish type. Of the wagon-roofs of the aisles, consideration will be deferred until we come to that of the roofing of the whole church.

According to Roscarrock, the shrine of St Endelienta was removed, at the time of its desecration during the reign of Henry VIII, from its original site, which was probably under the archway of the easternmost bay of the north aisle, to the middle of the easternmost bay of the south aisle, where it was placed in an east–west position over the remains of a parishioner (a Mrs Batten). In 1874, during the incumbency of the Reverend W. Hocken, it was placed in its present position, altarwise in the south chapel. Here it is seen to greater advantage. It must not, however, be regarded merely as a work of art. It is the shrine of a saint of whom it can be said that she worshipped the Lord 'in the beauty of holiness' and the beauty of her shrine should serve, not least, as a reminder of the sanctity of St Endelienta of whose possible 'presence' in the church mention has been made. The shrine has eight deep niches (three on the east and west sides, one on the north and south sides) which have ogee arches on colonnettes. These ogee arches match in miniature those in the bays of the aisles. Inside the niches are small vaults of great beauty. Nikolaus

Pevsner writes "The detail, such as the cusping, is as delicate as if it were of cast iron."[7] The shrine is the masterpiece of the 'Master of Endellion' and worthy of St Endelienta.

The chancel is spacious, simple and dignified. The high altar stands out against a background of plain fabric covering the east wall. The altar rails and the prebendal stalls, of Austrian oak, are of simple design. Some of the former altar rails (late seventeenth century) were incorporated into the present pulpit by Prebendary Murphy, Rector of the parish, during whose incumbency the excellent and extensive restoration of the church (1937–8) was carried out.

The north chapel, known as the Roscarrock Chapel, contains the tombstone of John Roscarrock (sixteenth century) whose descendant, Nicholas Roscarrock, heads the list of hagiographers of St Endelienta. In the north wall of the chapel is a stone staircase which gave access to the rood-screen which was unfortunately dismantled.

At the western end of the north aisle is a moveable screen constructed in 1901 to commemorate the death of Queen Victoria. Beyond it, the space is utilized to serve as a vestry.

The church possesses an Elizabethan chalice and paten made by More of Exeter. The chalice, however, is on a later stem. The 1549 Inventories of Church Goods, Exchequer (KR) Church Goods (E.117), File 1, No.51, has the following entry for the parish:

The p'ishe of Delyon.

The said p'ishners have ij chalises p'cell gylt It'm in ther tower iiij belles.

Crosses j.
Sm. the chalices xix.
Pixes ij.[8]
Sm. the belles xlj.
Balle of silv' j.[9]

[7] *The Buildings of England, Cornwall*, p.169.

[8] Pixes were used for the reservation of the Blessed Sacrament and were usually kept hanging beneath a tent-like canopy of fabric over the high altar.

[9] A "ball of silver" is mentioned in the inventory for Bodmin. In that for Liskeard a "silver shrine" is mentioned. The latter was probably a reliquary. Is it possible that the "balls of silver" at St Endellion and Bodmin were reliquaries?

The Marian Returns (1553) showing plate received from churches, plate returned to churches, and defaced plate delivered to the Jewel House–Exchequer (KR) Church Goods (E.117), No.12/42–have the following entry for the parish:

Endellion Received ther ij challis wt pates of … xvij onces di xvij onces di whereof one of them defacyd of vj onces di & ye rest redeliv'd

These entries are of interest. The commission for making Inventories (1549) in the reign of Edward VI was followed by others. That issued in 1553 (16th January) ordered the seizure of all parish plate, only the barest essential vessels being left for the use of the parish churches. The plate was to be sent to the Jewel House of the Tower of London and melted down. Edward VI died whilst this collection was proceeding. On the accession of Mary I an order was issued which provided for the return of church plate. Only that which had been defaced was to be sent to the Jewel House. The plate at St Endellion in the 1549 Inventory was two chalices (PG), one cross, two pixes and one ball of silver. In the Marian Returns, mention is made of two chalices with patens (17½ oz.). The Church of St Endellion, having had its shrine desecrated, according to Roscarrock, in the reign of Henry VIII, would seem to have been despoiled of cross, two pixes and a "ball of silver" in that of Edward VI.

We have almost completed our perambulation of the interior of the church. If we stand at the west end of the church and look east the glory of the original wagon-roofs is revealed. Fortunately they escaped those overzealous nineteenth-century restorers who were not blessed with any aesthetic sense. They contented themselves with a veritable riot of varnished pitch-pine. One example of their fervour for removal and replacement must suffice. The Jacobean pulpit was sold to the Roman Catholic church in Bodmin and replaced by a pitch-pine monstrosity. The roofing, however, was spared and during the 1937–8 restoration of the church, to which reference has already been made, the wagon-roofs were carefully taken down, restored and re-erected. During this work, a medieval rafter was brought to light with the date 1675 inscribed upon it. This points to a previous restoration in the seventeenth century which, like that of 1937–8, preserved the main structure of the original roofs. With the exception of a few of the originals, to which they are worthy successors, the guardian angels against the wall plates are the work of local carvers during the 1937–8 restoration when the roof bosses were also replaced, with the exception of three originals in the south aisle.

Our vantage point from which to look up at the roofing is adjacent to the entry to the tower. The tower contains a tourist's attraction which might vie, for example, with the Mermaid at Zennor. It is a delightful painting, on a board, of some bell-ringers in Georgian attire together with an equally delightful rhyme, which ends:

And since bells are for modest recreation
Let's rise and ring and fall to admiration.

These lines alone would form an appropriate motto for bell-ringers everywhere. The tower contains a peal of six bells (two more than in the 1549 Inventory) which were recast in 1734 and, again, in 1952.

We began our perambulation at the holy water stoup. We end it at the font, in the south aisle and to the right of the south door, as we leave the church. The font is Norman (*c.* 1150) and although it is very plain it is very important for it is evidence that the present church replaced an earlier building.

As it would be unwise to claim a pre-Norman origin for the Collegiate Church of St Endelienta it may only be said that the earlier building was probably erected in the mid-twelfth century (on the evidence of the existing font–*c.* 1150) though there is no documentary mention of St Endellion Church until 1260.

The building of the present fifteenth-century church may have been necessary because of the state of the fabric of the earlier building. Evidence of this possibility may perhaps be provided from the 1331 visitation of churches in the Diocese of Exeter during the episcopate of John de Grandison.[10] Those in

[10] Bishop of Exeter from 1327–1369. He succeeded James de Berkeley whose episcopate began and ended in 1327. He, in turn, succeeded Walter de Stapeldon (1308–26) of whom mention must be made because he was the founder of Stapeldon Hall in Oxford (1314) soon after to be known as Exeter College, Oxford members of which foundation are to be found in the lists of the Prebends of St Endellion.

Cornwall would seem to have been considered the worst neglected. Of sixteen churches or chapels therein of only one could it be said that "all is in a good state, as it seems, for the present". The chancel in three churches was considered more or less ruinous and in eleven churches the books and furniture were in a scandalously bad state. Perhaps St Endellion was not the exception and fell into either of the other categories. Be that as it may, of the present fifteenth-century church it can be said that in the twentieth century "all is in good state" omitting the cautious rider of 1331 "as it seems, for the present".

As to other places of worship in the parish which were associated with the cult of St Endelienta mention must be made after we have turned to the identity of the Saint herself and her place in the Calendar of that company of Cornish saints who lived in what has been called the Age of the Saints.

The Family of St Endelienta, V.

The scholarly Guibert de Nogent wrote a treatise *c.* 1120 entitled *The Relics of the Saints* in which he extolled those saints whose existence was "for reverence and honour, for the saints' example and protection".[1] He deplored, at the same time, the many alleged saints who were not real ones.

Evidence of the existence of such saints may be found among the treasures of the Collegiate Church of St Peter, Westminster. It houses a stone statue of a female saint, bearded and wearing withal a moustache. Traditionally known as Wilgefortis, she was affectionately nicknamed Uncumber in England.[2] Her prayers were asked by unhappily married medieval ladies who, forbidden the remedy of divorce, sought her aid to uncumber them of their husbands.

St Endelienta, it is hoped to demonstrate, was a real saint but to establish her identity and her connection with the Collegiate Church of St Endelienta, where she has long been venerated, the modern hagiographer has to sift through a considerable amount of information concerning her some of which is conflicting or confusing. In this task he is aided or hindered, as the case may be, by former hagiographers.

Before trying to place St Endelienta in her rightful niche in the Celtic Church in Cornwall, it would seem useful to take a bird's-eye view of Celtic Cornwall with the aid of historical geographers and archaeologists whose labours have brought to light much valuable information of great assistance to the researches of hagiographers.

The Cornish Peninsular was strategically placed on the Western Seaways[3] in Prehistoric and Proto-historic times.

[1] *Patrologia Latina,* ed. J.P. Migne. CLVI de Pignoribus sanctorum, cols 607–80 (Paris 1878–90). Guibert de Nogent, a pupil of Anselm of Bec, became Abbot of Nogent.

[2] Wilgefortis acquired the additional name of Liberata (the deliverer) with variations of it, e.g. Regenfledis (Flemish) and Ontkommer, Kummernis (German), but the Anglicized version is surely the most delightful.

[3] These comprised what are today known as the Bay of Biscay, the English Channel, St George's Channel, the Irish Sea and the North Channel.

Shipping from Spain, for example, would proceed north past Brittany and Cornwall, separated by the Mare Austrum, and then enter the Mare Occidentale on its way to Wales, Ireland, the Isle of Man and further north. There were also transpeninsular routes across Cornwall which avoided the stormy promontory of Lands End and the Lizard and which were convenient for commerce in tin. Two of these routes were from Fowey to Harlyn Bay and from St Ives to St Michael's Mount which was a notable depot for Cornish tin. The Western English Channel, the Mare Austrum, was also known as the Muir'n Icht or the Sea of Icht (after *ictis*–mount).

The sea and transpeninsular routes would have conveyed other commodities as well as tin. Such luxuries as wine and oil from Mediterranean lands would have been sought by the inhabitants of the north-western Celtic lands. There would have been passengers as well. Later, in the Age of the Saints, these peregrini would have included in their number the missionary saints.

The Western Seaways made contact possible between the Gallic, Spanish and Mediterranean world and the inhabitants of Wales, Ireland, the Isle of Man and, further afield, those of the Galloway Peninsular and the Solway region. Cornwall might be said to have been situated at the centre of things and of particular importance were the transpeninsular routes across it not only for commerce and culture but, later on in the Age of the Saints, for Celtic Christianity. This centrality, too, meant that it was roughly equidistant from Wales and Brittany with which, together with Ireland, it was to have strong links in all three respects.

Prehistoric and Proto-historic Britain may be considered as having consisted culturally of three provinces. The Inner Province lay in the region south and east of a line drawn roughly from the Wash to the Dorset coast. The Intermediate formed a corridor, so to say, from East Yorkshire in the north to Somerset and Gloucestershire in the south. The Outer consisted of the rest of the British Isles and of this Province we are concerned with Ireland, Wales and Cornwall.[4]

[4] For this division of Britain into cultural provinces I am indebted to A. Downes whose unpublished thesis *The Prehistoric and Proto-historic Culture Areas of Britain* is quoted

In our quest for St Endelienta we are also concerned with Brittany and we must now select, over a considerable period of time, evidence of some of the links between all four regions.

In the third century B.C. the Western Sea routes brought over into Cornwall the La Tene culture from Western France. Cornish tin may well have been the attraction which prompted its arrival. The La Tene culture spread to Wales. So we have an early link between Brittany, Wales and Cornwall.

During the period immediately prior to the Roman invasion of Britain it would seem that the tin trade was in the hands of the Veneti. These were experienced seamen and skilled withal in the art of defences as evidenced, for example, by their erection of cliff castles. Examples of these fortifications are to be found at Gunnards Head in Penwith (Cornwall), at Kercaradoc and Penhars near Quimper (Brittany) and in the Gower Peninsular (Wales).

Much later (from the fifth to the seventh centuries A.D.) evidence of Irish settlements in South-Western Wales and Cornwall is provided by Ogham[5] stones.

Before turning to their significance and, for our purpose, to one of them in particular, a digression must be made concerning the Irish invasion of, and consequent settlement in, South-West Wales. Legendary accounts of events from sources of a later age emanating from Wales, Ireland, Cornwall and Brittany may help us. Shorn of fantasy and fiction these, to borrow mathematical terms, may be said to have a highest common factor or a lowest common multiple, as the case may be, which produce information which is at least likely and intelligible though it is not a little confusing in parts and must be used with great caution.

The Irish invasion of South-West Wales took place towards the end of the fifth century. The traditions of Cardigan lead us to suppose a landing on the coast there *c.* 490 by an Irish chief Broca or Brocagnus who was accompanied by an Irish King of Demetia and a company of captains bearing Munster names.

in E.G. Bowen's *Saints, Seaways and Settlements* from which I have gratefully obtained much information.

[5] Ogham, a script based on the Latin alphabet, consists of consonants and vowels represented by long and short strokes cut in stone.

The traditions of Glamorgan would have us believe that King Arthur came to the Usk in which case if his famous battle at Urbs Legionis were not at Chester it might possibly have been at Usk at Caerleon. Another Glamorgan legend makes Arthur wage war with one Brychan and check the latter's advance along the Roman road from Cardiff to Brecon.

The Irish settlement, following the invasion of Wales, in Southern Breconshire is of great interest because this region takes its name from that eponymous King of Brecon–Brychan who was possibly the prolific Brychan whose many children produced many a saint. There were, of course, many Brychans. It was quite a common Irish name. This Brychan may have been the son of that Broca or Brocagnus, the Irish chief mentioned above. If this were the case it is a moot point whether it was the father or his son who engaged in warfare with Arthur.

The Brecon legends mention one Theodoric, a captain in Arthur's army, memories of whom extend to Cornwall and Brittany.[6] Cornish tradition gives Theodoric a lordship south of the Padstow estuary. North of the Padstow estuary are the parishes of Trigg named after the daughters of Brychan. East of the Padstow–Camel estuary there was an Irish infiltration via the Irish settlers of South Wales. In the Age of the Saints there was a migration from South Wales and Cornwall into Brittany.

With this miscellaneous information in mind we may now return to the Ogham stones and find among them an archaeological starting-point in our quest for St Endelienta.

Ogham-inscribed memorial stones originated in Ireland where the distribution of them is concentrated in the south and where they are monolingual informing the beholder of them that he was looking at the stone of 'X' the son or daughter of 'Y'. These monoliths would be found on the highways approaching centres of population and where there were cemeteries they would mark the grave of some person of

[6] It is most unfortunate that the early vernacular literature of Cornwall and of Brittany has perished. Later Cornish traditions would seem to include Theodoric, representative of many an unknown soldier, by chance. His death in a hunting accident in the Falmouth region, where he would seem to have had another lordship, is given between 530 and 550.

importance. From Ireland they spread to South Wales and Cornwall. There are some ninety examples in South Wales, one third of which are bilingual, i.e. in Latin as well as in Ogham script. In Dumnonia some fifty stones have so far been discovered. Five bilingually inscribed stones are known in Cornwall, viz. two at Lewannick and one at St Kew, Worthyvale and St Endellion.[7]

Canon Taylor[8] mentions that at St Endellion: "There is an interesting inscribed stone at Doyden Head which formerly stood at the crossroads midway between Endellion and Port Quin. The inscription as deciphered by the late Rev. William Jago, reads: BROEGAN HIC JACIT NADOTTI FILIUS. Brokannus is William of Worcester's equivalent of Brychan, St Endelienta's father. Can Endellion claim to be the last resting place of the great Brychan himself?"

This reading differs slightly from that given in the *Victoria History of the County of Cornwall*,[9] also provided by William Jago, which is "BROGAGNI HIC IACIT NADOTTI FILIUS" and is preceded by the Chi-Rho mongram. This is the correct reading which translated records that Brocagnus lies here, the son of Nadottus. The date of the monolith is probably sixth or seventh century, i.e. within the dating of all the inscribed stones in Cornwall at earliest about the beginning of the fifth century and at latest the end of the eighth.

We must now try and answer the question posed by Canon Taylor–can Endellion claim to be the last resting place of the Great Brychan himself? It has to be admitted, at the outset, that Brychan is as elusive as St Endelienta, 'the mysterious Brychan' as he has been called.

There is a short Latin tract, the *Cognatio de Brychan*, of which there are two versions which widely differ. The *De situ Brecheniauc* (Cottonian Collection Vespasian A xiv) is an early thirteenth century work written in the vicinity of Brecon but copied from an earlier manuscript. The other (Cottonian Collection Domitian i) was written *c.* 1650 but is merely an indifferent copy of an earlier manuscript.

[7] The St Clement stone is inscribed, it would seem, in Latin only.

[8] *St Endellion Prebendal Church; Its Constitution and History*. Truro, 1929.

[9] Vol I, p.420. Published 1924.

From this source we learn of Marchell, daughter of King Tewdrig, who married Anlach by whom she had a son called Brychan who was born at Benni near Brecon. Brychan was fostered by Drichan, a Christian sage, from whom he received instruction in the Faith. Eventually, Brychan was handed over by Anlach as a hostage to the King of Powys whose daughter, Banadlinet, was violated by Brychan as a result of which she gave birth to a son called Cynog.

This parentage of Brychan conflicts with that of Broca or Brocagnus, the Irish chief who invaded Wales *c*. 490. Whatever his parentage, however, a King Brychan, blessed with many children (all, or most of whom, became saints), figures in Irish, Welsh, Breton and Cornish hagiology. Brychan's identity is obscured by various traditions but, whoever he was, he had a daughter, St Endelienta.

The *Cognatio de Brychan* (CC Vesp. A xiv) lists eleven sons and twenty-five daughters of Brychan. Among the latter is Kenethon. In the later Welsh lists Kenethon appears as Cyneiddon together with Cenedlon. Whether Kenethon is the same person as Cenedlon is open to doubt but there is no doubt that Cenedlon is St Endelienta. The *Cognatio* (CC Dom. i) records that Brychan was buried "in mynav in valle que dicitur vall Brychan" which might be anywhere.

The copyist who produced this version of the *Cognatio c.* 1650 worked from a manuscript (probably of thirteenth-century date) which he would seem to have been unable to read with any great degree of proficiency. One is tempted to translate "in my(nav) in valle que dicitur vall Brychan" as "a field in a valley/hollow called the valley/hollow of Brychan". Everything hinges on the word 'my(nav)'.[10] It might possibly be a corruption of the Latin *arvum*, almost forming an anagram. Coincidentally the Cornish word 'my' means a field.

If this interpretation warrants cautious acceptance, then Endellion could, at least, lay claim to be the last resting place of Brychan. Such a claim would be weakened by the reference to Nadottus, who by no stretch of the imagination could be

[10] Possibly 'mynav' is a corrupt form of 'Mannia' in Scotland but the Ogham stone is in Cornwall.

identified with either Anlach[11] or Broca. On the other hand, the claim would be strengthened by the Ogham stone being sited in the place where St Endelienta, daughter of Brychan, lived and died.

The identity of St Endelienta's mother poses a further problem. The *Cognatio* claims that Brychan had three wives; the earlier version names them as Prawst, Rhibrawst and Proistri; the later as Eurbrawst, Rhybrawst and Proestri. Be this as it may, it would seem simplest to accept none of these ladies, whose claim to the motherhood of St Endelienta it is impossible to substantiate, but rather to regard Gladwisa, on the evidence of the *Life of St Nectan* (Gotha MS M.n. 57), as the mother of St Endelienta.

There are not a few lists of the Children of Brychan from various sources, Welsh, Breton, Irish and Cornish, some of which are enumerated below (a selection must needs suffice) and two of which we shall consider synoptically[12]

Here, then, in chronological order, is a selection of the lists:

1. That given in the *Life of St Nectan* (Gotha MS. M.n.57) Date: end of 12th century. (24 sons and daughters.)
2. *De Situ Brecheniauc.* A Latin MS *c.* 1200. (25 sons and daughters.) Brychan has three wives, cf. the *Cognatio Brychan.* Gwladus (Gladwisa) is named as his daughter and not as his wife.
3. The *Cognatio Brychan* (CC Vesp. A xiv) Date: early 13th century. (11 sons and 25 daughters.)
4. Jesus College, Oxford MS 20. Date: early 15th century. (11 sons and 24 daughters.)
5. William of Worcester's list. Date: 1478. William Botoner (his mother's maiden name), as he indiscriminately called himself, was a great traveller and keeper of notebooks.

[11] *Cognatio* (CC Vesp. A xiv) names Anlac/Anlach/Anlauch as the son of Coronac; *Cognatio* (CC Dom. i) names Anlach as son of Gormac; a Jesus College, Oxford MS 20 names "Chormuc, son of Eubre the Goidel, of Ireland" as the father of Brychan. A pedigree of Brychan from Caelbadh, King of Ulster is given by Shearman (*Loca Patriciana*) which was adopted by the Bollandists but this is discountenanced by both the Leabhar Breac and the Leabhar Genealach.

[12] For elucidation of the intricacy of some of the lists the reader should refer to Canon G.H. Doble's *S.Nectan, S.Keyne and the Children of Brychan in Cornwall* and to Part V of his work on *The Saints of Cornwall* (St Nectan).

These covered a wide range of interests. His itinerary through Cornwall in 1478 extended from Launceston to St Michael's Mount via Bodmin and he paid visits to the most important religious houses en route. His eagle eye never failed to examine the various Kalendars and Martyrologies and he made enquiries concerning the Celtic saints commemorated in place names. (24 children.)

6. John Leland's list. Date: first half of 16th century. This antiquary (*c.* 1506–52) in the space of six years collected "a whole world of things very memorable". During his visit to Cornwall he must have had the sight of the same documentary evidence of the Children of Brychan as that seen by William of Worcester either at Bodmin or Launceston and most likely at the latter place.
7. Nicholas Roscarrock's list. Date: late 16th century. Roscarrock, the friend of the antiquary William Camden and his contemporary, was assisted in the compilation of the longest list of the Children of Brychan (32 sons and 31 daughters) by a Welsh priest (Edward Powell) and its comparative lack of usefulness to us is redeemed by his having provided a brief biography of St Endelienta which is of the greatest aid to us in our quest for the saint.
8. The *Cognatio Brychan* (CC Dom. i) Date: *c.* 1650. (13 sons and 24 daughters.)
9. The Iolo MSS. provide three lists:
   p.111 from a Coychurch MS. Date: 1670. (24 sons and 26 daughters.)
   pp.119–21 from another Coychurch MS. (25 sons and 26 daughters.)
   p.140 from a Cardiff MS (25 sons and 28 daughters.)
10. The Cambro-British Saints, pp. 270–71, from Harleian MS. Date: early 18th century. (2 sons and 20 daughters.)

The number of children which Brychan is supposed to have fathered in these various lists ranges from two to thirty-one sons and from eleven to thirty-one daughters. An early reference to the number of daughters comes from Giraldus Cambrensis (*c.* 1147–*c.* 1223), the Norman-Welsh historian, who, in his *Itinerarium Cambriae*, regarded Brychan as "a powerful and noble personage" and observed that "the British histories testified that he had four-and-twenty daughters, all of whom, dedicated from their youth to religious observances, happily ended their lives in sanctity".

Thomas Fuller (1608–61), the antiquary, historian and divine, mentioned Brychan in his *Worthies of England* and also observed that "This King had four-and-twenty daughters, a jolly number; and all of them saints, a greater happiness". He also has this to say of Cornwall in his *Church History of Britain*: "That county is the Cornucopia of saints, (most of Irish extraction,) and the names of their towns and villages the best nomenclature of the devout men of this age [i.e. the sixth century]." He continues: "If the people of that province have as much holiness in their hearts, as the parishes therein carry sanctity in their names, Cornwall may pass for another Holy Land in public reputation."

THE CHILDREN OF BRYCHAN

Life of St. Nectan (Gotha MS)	*William of Worcester's List*	*Places where the saint is commemorated*
Nectan	Nectanus	Hartland, Welcombe, Ashcombe, Chulmleigh, St Nighton's Chapel near St Winnow, St Nighton's Kieve near Tintagel, St Nectan, near Lostwithiel
John	Johannes	Instow (John's Stow), St John's Well in Morwenstow; there is a possible connection with Ploujean, Brittany
Endelient	Endelient	St Endellion
Menfre	Menfrede	St Minver
Dilic	Dilit	Commemorated at Port Isaac, where there was a mediaeval chapel of St Electa. There is a St Illec in Brittany.
Tedda	Tedda	St Teath

Mabon	Maben	St Mabyn
Merewenne	Marwenna	Marhamchurch; possibly at St Merryn, near Padstow
Wenna	Wenna	St Wenn, also Patron of Morval, near Looe; there is also the site of a chapel of St Wenna in St Kew parish
Juliana	Julliana	There is St Juliot near Boscastle; Charles Henderson tells us of Lanteglos by Camelford as being known as Ecclesia Sancte Julitte in 1288
Wynup	Wymip	The name suggests Gwennap styled St Weneppa in 1281 (Charles Henderson)
Wenheden	Wenheden	There is a St Eden in Brittany. Charles Henderson suggested Wenheden should be Wenhedec–Guenedoc, now St Enodock near St Minver
Wencu	Wencu	Possibly St Kew. The Celtic name of this place was Lan-Docco after the founder of the Monastery of Docco which St Samson visited in the 6th century. St Kew, patroness of a chapel there, superseded St Docco and since *c*. 1440 the parish has been named after her
Wensent	Wensent	Probably Lezant if Wensent is St Sant, an eponym
Cleder	Cleder	St Clether
Keri	Kery	Egloskerry
Jona	Jona	Now unknown in Cornwall but his name appears in *Vita Samsonis* as King of Domnonia in Brittany and in the genealogy of St Winnoc. St Winnow is situated in the vicinity of the Brychan parishes in South Cornwall
Helie	Helye	Difficult to identify. He might

		be the eponym of Llanelyw. Elyw is said to have been a granddaughter of Brychan. The parishes called Egloshayle may derive from Eglos Helye
Canauc	Kananc	Difficult to identify. Ecton (Thesaurus) says St Knet is patron of Lesnewth. St Knet may be a corrupt form of Kananc. Wade-Evans suggests Kananc denotes Kanauc, i.e. Cynog
Kenhender	Kerhender	Wade-Evans suggests Cynidr, grandson of Brychan
Adwen	Adwenhelye	Advent near Camelford. William of Worcester may have added 'helye' by mistake
Tamalanc	Tamalanc	Perhaps Talland, the Mother Church of West Looe, is a corruption of the name
Yse	Yse	St Issey and Mevagissey
Morewenna	Morwenna	Morwenstow

The saints on these two lists and the places where they are commemorated show St Endelienta surrounded by members of her family in the vicinity of the Camel estuary and northwards. We must bear in mind, however, that other members of her family are commemorated in the vicinity of the Fowey and Looe estuaries. Only a few of these saints are mentioned in the above lists.

For information concerning other Children of Brychan in South Cornwall we must turn to the Latin MS *c.* 1200: *De Situ Brecheniauc.* This names Cain–St Keyne[13]–eponym of the parish of that name, a female or male itinerant missionary who was also the original patron of St Martin's-by-Looe; Berwin or Berwyn whom Wade-Evans identifies as Barry, patron of

[13] For St Keyne, the reader should refer to Canon Doble's *S.Nectan, S.Keyne and the Children of Brychan in Cornwall.* Part II (Cornish Saints Series No. 25). The latter has a bonus for it incorporates Notes on the cult of St. Nectan by Charles Henderson.

Fowey; "Rydoch, i. Judoc, filius Brachan in Francia" probably eponym of Lanredoch, now Lanreath. Adjacent to Lanreath is Pelynt, probably a curious corruption of Plou-Nonnita (*De Situ Brecheniauc* names Nunyd or Ninid as a daughter of Brychan).

Reference has been made to the transpeninsular routes used by merchants. Among the missionary saints who also used them the Children of Brychan, the Family of St Endelienta, contributed not a few. We must now turn to the life of St Endelienta, not the least of a notable saintly band.

St Endelienta, V.

In the Parish Church of St Neot (Cornwall), almost as famous as Fairford (Gloucestershire) for its stained glass, there is a window which possibly depicts St Brychan, haloed and crowned, seated on a throne and enfolding on his lap ten of his children. M.D. Anderson, who makes mention of this window in her informative book *Looking for History in British Churches,*[1] p. 50, adds, however, that it was probably a nineteenth-century restorer's misconception of a medieval representation apropos All Saints and, by way of comparison, she calls to mind an illuminated initial for All Saints' Day in a psalter to be seen in the Fitzwilliam Museum, Cambridge.[2] Nikolaus Pevsner describes the window as depicting "God with Souls in his lap" and informs us that the fifteenth-century and early sixteenth-century glass at St Neot was much restored and renewed by John Hedgeland *c.* 1830.

It would be nice to be able to assert positively that the window is, indeed, a delightful representation of St Brychan holding some of his children but we do not have sufficient evidence to support such a claim. It will be recalled that we have a similar difficulty over the Ogham Stone in the Parish of St Endellion which possibly commemorates St Endelienta's saintly father.

In attempting a new biography of his daughter there are one or two assertions that can be made with some degree of confidence after which we must content ourselves with trying to picture the sort of person she was and the sort of life she led.

That St Endelienta was a daughter of 'the mysterious Brychan' is established by the references to her as Cenedlon and Endelient in some of the lists of the Children of Brychan. It seems very likely that she lived during the sixth century. That

[1] First published by John Murray (1951).
[2] M.R. James: Catalogue of MSS in the Fitzwilliam Museum, No. 34, p. 88.
[3] *The Buildings of England: Cornwall,* 2nd Edition, by Nikolaus Pevsner, revised by Enid Radcliffe, pp. 197–8. Penguin Books.

she lived and died in the place to which she gave her name is certain. It was customary for the Celtic Church to dedicate a place of worship to its founder, who also gave his or her name to the locality in which such a building was situated.

The original centre of worship dedicated to St Endelienta would probably have been built of wood or wattle. Of this building we have, as yet, no archaeological evidence.[4] It was sited in delightful scenery the features of which we can observe and enjoy today. It served a small agricultural community. Evidence of its population is probably provided by the Domesday Book (1086) for although this survey was made five centuries after that in which St Endelienta lived it is unlikely that the population then was either larger or smaller to any great extent. The following statistics from Domesday Book relating to four places in what became the Parish of St Endellion are of interest:

Place	*Slaves*	*Villagers*	*Small-holders*	*Animals*	*Land*
Roscarrock	4	2	5	4 cattle 4 pigs 30 sheep 1 mare	Meadow: 1 acre; land for 4 ploughs
Trefreock	1	2	3	3 cattle 40 sheep	Pasture: 20 acres; land for 2 ploughs
Kilmarth	1		3	40 sheep	Pasture: 10 acres; land for 1 plough
Trewethart		1			Land for 2 ploughs

To picture the sort of person she was we must turn to the biography of St Endelienta written by Nicholas Roscarrock.[5]

[4] The recent discovery of an ancient burial ground in the vicinity of the present church may produce such evidence. We await the archaeologist's report.

[5] The DNB describes him as "a Roman catholic and versifier, born probably about 1549". The Registrum Coll.Exon.Oxon. Part II (C.W.Boase) has the entry: "Roscharocke, Nicholas, sup. B.A. 3 May 1568, at Inner Temple 1571, as of Roscarrock, Cornwall". He was an ardent Catholic recusant. This resulted in his imprisonment in the Tower (1580–86) where he was racked in 1581. In 1593 he was again in prison but in the Fleet. From 1607 he lived at Haworth Castle where he was possibly tutor to Lord William Howard's sons and where he died in 1633 or 1634. The late Charles Henderson, in his unpublished MS notes, tells us that Roscarrock's *Lives of Saints* (800

He tells us, on the evidence of the *Life of St Nectan*, that she was the daughter of the well-known (if "often named" may be so rendered) St Brychan by his wife Gladwisa. This we have established. Then he provides some new and valuable information. She lived, he says, at Trentinney and he recalls that a chapel, as he supposed, dedicated to her had existed and, although destroyed at the time he wrote, was commemorated by a place called Chapel Close, south-west of the parish church, also dedicated to her, marking the site of the chapel which, in its turn, marked the site of Trentinney. Here she lived, he goes on to say, a very austere life.

After providing us with this important information, for which there was evidence, he relates some legends concerning St Endelienta. Before considering these it might be wise to consult Guibert de Nogent's *Treatise on Relics c.* 1120 (Book I, Chapter i, Col. 614). Guibert was critical of popular canonization. Having in mind "the common folk of our towns and villages" he says: "Let them tell me how they can expect a man to be their patron saint concerning whom they know not even that which is to be known? For thou shalt find no record of him but his mere name. Yet, while the clergy hold their peace, old wives and herds of base wenches chant the lying legends of such patron saints....". The scholarly Guibert's strictures, however, cannot be said to apply in their entirety to St Endelienta. We know who she was and that she was known by the people among whom she lived. Nevertheless, the legends concerning her must be considered criticially and with caution.

Roscarrock relates that she restricted her diet to the milk from her cow. This would have been in character with her austere way of life. Similar examples of saintly austerity are not

closely written pages) was mainly based on earlier writers such as Capgrave and Father Whitford and compiled at Haworth. Henderson calls the *Life of St Endelienta* a "small and precious pearl in a great shell". "Roscarrock," he says, "knew Cornwall in boyhood before the old ceremonies, customs and religious observances had been swept away for ever by the accession of Elizabeth 1558. It is for local information from this district [St Agnes and Tintagel] that his book has real value and without which it would be of little interest. It is to local tradition that he owes his interesting accounts of such saints as St Endelienta" :MS ADD.3041 ULC). Roscarrock was baptized in St Endellion Church of which his family were benefactors.

unknown from St John the Baptist onwards. The sixth-century Welsh monk St Decuman, Patron Saint of Watchet, near Dunster, in Somerset also possessed a cow from which he too may well have provided himself with a meagre diet.

That St Endelienta's animal strayed on to the land of the Lord of Trentinney was a natural thing for it to have done. Its slaughter by an irate landowner is plausible and puts him in a bad light as far as his feeling for the animal and its owner are concerned. That the Godfather of St Endelienta should be shocked by such a callous act was a natural reaction but that he killed, or caused to be killed, the owner of the property on which St Endelienta's cow had strayed is highly improbable.

The identification of St Endelienta's Godfather with King Arthur is intriguing. If Brychan's father was the Irish chieftain who took part in an invasion of Wales *c.* 490 and if he, or his son, did wage war with Arthur and afterwards, let us say, came to terms with him, then we have a possible clue as to how the legend arose that Arthur was Godfather to St Endelienta.

The miraculous restoration to life of the Lord of Trentinney by St Endelienta is equally highly improbable. There is no evidence that St Endelienta worked miracles at Trentinney nor that they have been sworn to have taken place at her shrine. It suffices to regard her as an intercessor rather than a worker of miracles during her lifetime and after her death.

Roscarrock tells us that when she knew that her death was imminent she "intreated her friends" to make certain arrangements for her burial. He describes how they were carried out in such a moving way that they have a ring of truth about them. The carrying of her body on a sledge drawn by young animals to a place at which these stopped of their own accord indicating where she was to be buried and where her shrine was to be built is analogous to the funeral arrangements of many early saints whose lives and deaths have been surrounded by legends.[6]

[6] In the case of St Ronan (to cite one example), buried at Locronan in Brittany, the funeral procession was interrupted. As the pair of oxen drawing a wagon which conveyed the saint's body approached the place of its burial they were attacked by the wife of a peasant. Her husband, it seems, had often visited the saint for religious instruction. She considered her husband's attendance upon the saint a dereliction of

Roscarrock adds to his brief biography of St Endelienta the date of her Feast (29th April), mentions her association with Lundy Island,[7] inserts his Poem to his Patroness, refers to two holy wells in the Parish of St Endellion[8] and, finally, tells us about the Saint's tomb.[9]

The particulars of her life are as elusive as those of her father's. The facts which have been established concerning her existence together with the legends which grew up about her enable us to form a picture of the sort of person she was. One might say that she was someone whose poverty and austerity, whose love of people and animals in a small agricultural community, whose simplicity and sanctity springing from her devotion and dedication to God influenced those among whom she lived and who regarded her as a holy person. Simple (in the spiritual connotation which may be given to that word) people are given grace to recognize sanctity and the popular canonization which St Endelienta was accorded, sooner or later, was undoubtedly a reflection of the Divine.

For the sort of life which St Endelienta led we must turn our attention to Celtic monasticism. A lengthy digression into early monasticism is beyond the scope of this essay but it is necessary for our purpose to make a brief reference to it.

In the Early Church there were groups of Christians practising disciplined lives of prayer and sanctity who revealed their faith in such charitable works as the visitation of the sick and the distribution of alms. They might be said to have performed

his domestic duties and dreaded lest he be drawn to desert her for the monastic life. Her malice towards St Ronan was such that she tried to ward off the animals carrying his body to his grave. Her attempt was thwarted. This sixth-century saint rests in his sixteenth-century tomb at Lochronan.

[7] A chapel was dedicated to St Endelienta on Lundy Island but we have no evidence of her ever having visited this place. It is situated twelve miles north-west of Hartland where her brother, St Nectan, is commemorated.

[8] In pre-Christian times wells were looked upon with wonder. Water, one of the four constituent elements of the Earth, was essential to life. Primitive people believed that some mysterious power caused springs of water to well forth and that indwelling spirits possessed powers of divination and healing. Holy wells owed their sanctity to the prayers and presence of local saints. Of these at St Endellion only one (just over a quarter of a mile from the church) can be identified but it is the more remote one that is said to have been frequented by St Endelienta.

[9] Roscarrock's biography, etc., is given in full on pp. 70–72.

their pastoral work as representatives of the local community of Christians with which they worshipped in public.

Possibly by A.D. 300, and perhaps even earlier, there emerged other groups of Christians leading equally dedicated and disciplined lives but who segregated themselves from the life of the local Christian community and retired to their own places of worship where they followed their own rule of life. Eusebius of Caesarea does not mention them in his important history of the Early Church. Such communities were not common before 330 but we know that they existed in Egypt and in Syria by 360.

There is a considerable amount of source material on the subject of early monasticism. The sayings attributed to hermits in the Egyptian desert are to be found in the famous *Apophthegmata.* There is a *Life of Antony* which is undoubtedly a document emanating from primitive Egyptian monasticism of which Antony was one of the founders. St Jerome wrote a *Life of the Hermit Paul*, another founder, and although this biography is what today would be called an historical novel it lays claim to include information derived from two disciples of Antony. A contemporary of Antony was Pachomius, who also has a biography, the founder of the famous monastery at Tabennisi.

Other sources are the *Historia Monachorum*, telling of visitors to the Egyptian solitaries during the last decade of the fourth century who may have come out of curiosity rather than to embrace the religious life and the Lausiac *History of Palladius* who, when he had been a bishop for twenty years, looked back on his experience as a monk in Egypt before beginning his episcopate. For information about fifth-century monasticism, however, our most helpful guide is the great Cassian whose visit to Egypt ended *c.* 400. His *Conferences* present us with the asceticism practised there.

The Egyptian monks lived in cells set apart at some distance from each other and in the case of Paphnutius, whose love of solitude earned him the name of the Buffalo, even further afield. In their cells they led lives of prayer and meditation upon the scriptures for the most part in silence but joining in a common act of prayer at the ninth hour though separated from

The Church interior

The Ogham stone bearing the inscription: BROGAGNI HIC IACIT NADOTTI FILIUS

The holy water stoup

The Shrine of St Endelienta

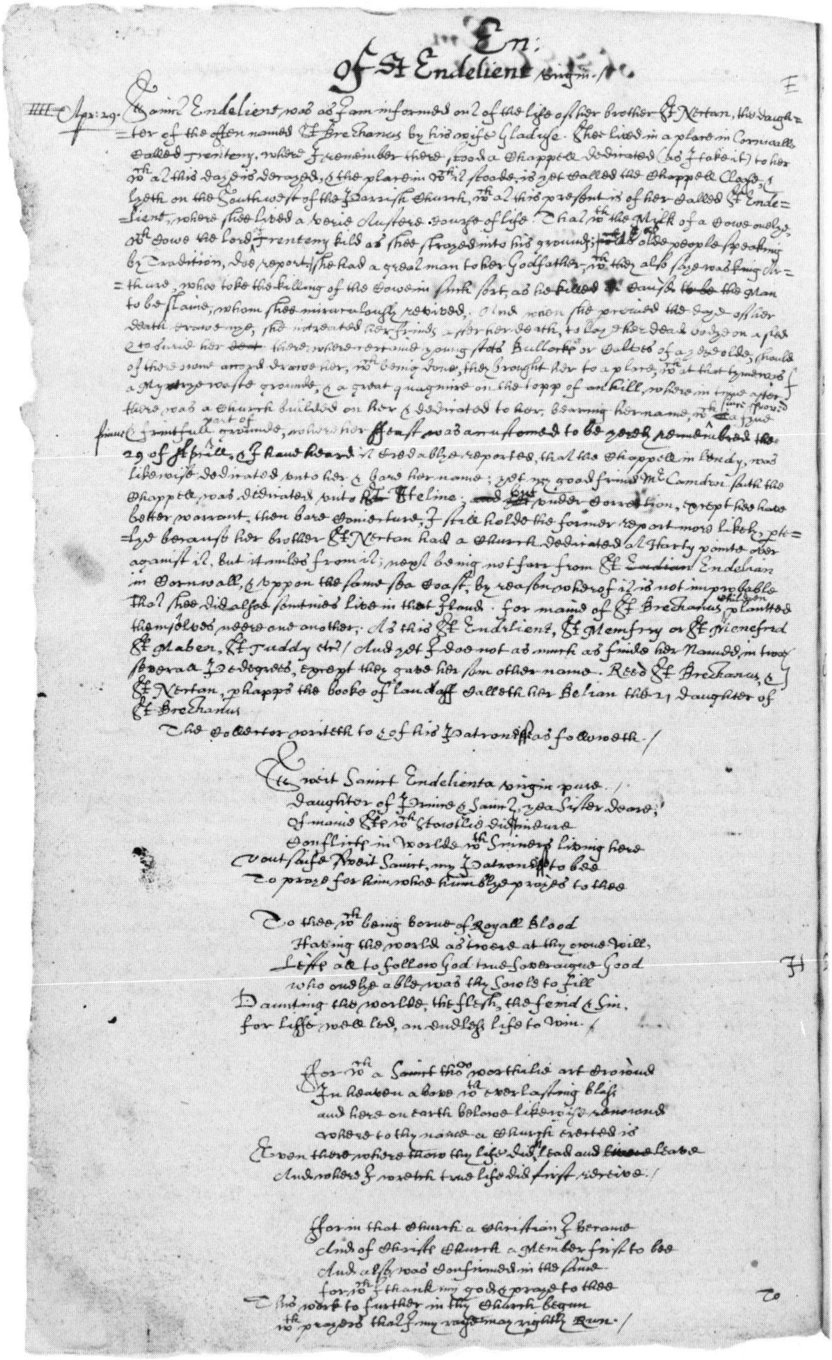

E

Of St Endelient Virgin etc.

Apr: 29. Saint Endelient, was as I am informed out of the life of her brother St Nectan, the daughter of the often named St Brechanus by his wife Gladuse. Shee lived in a place in Cornwall called Trentenny, where I remember there stood a Chappell dedicated (as I take it) to her which at this day is decayed, and the place in which it stood, is yet called the Chappell Close, and lyeth on the Southwest of the Parrish Church, which at this present is of her called St Endelient, where shee lived a verie Austere course of life. That with the Milk of a Cowe onelye which Cowe the lord of Trentenny kild as shee strayed into his ground; and the olde people speaking by tradition, doe report, she had a great man to her Godfather, which they also saye was king Arthure, who toke the killing of the Cowe in such sort, as he caused the man to be slaine, whom shee miraculously revived. And when she perceived the daye of her death drawe nye, she intreated her frinds after her death, to laye her dead bodye on a sled and to burie her there where certaine young stots Bullocks or Calves of a yeare olde, should of them selves draw her, which being done, they brought her to a place, which at that tyme was a Myrie waste grounde, and a great quagmire on the topp of an hill, where in tyme after there was a Church builded on her and dedicated to her, bearing her name, which since proved faire and fruitfull part of grounde, where her ffeast was accustomed to be yerely remembred the 29 of Aprill. I have heard it credablye reported, that the Chappell in Lundy, was likewise dedicated unto her and bare her name; yet my good frind Mr Camden saith the Chappell was dedicated unto St Helline, but under correction, except hee have better warrant, then bare Conjecture, I still holde the former report more likely, especially because her brother St Nectan had a Church dedicated at Harty pointe over against it, but 4 miles from it; which being not farr from St Endelian in Cornwall, and uppon the same sea coast, by reason whereof it is not improbable that shee did also sometimes live in that Iland. for manie of St Brechanus children planted themselves there one and another; As this St Endelient, St Menfry or St Menefred St Maben, St Teddy etc. And yet I doe not as much as finde her Named in two severall Pedegrees, except they gave her som other name. Reed St Brechanus and St Nectan, perhapps the booke of Landaff calleth her Belian there, daughter of St Brechanus

The Collector writeth to one of his Patronesses as followeth.

Thy wit Saint Endelienta virgin pure.
Daughter of Prince and Saint, yea Sister deare;
Of manie Sts which stoutlie did endure
Conflicts in worlde which Sinners living here
Vouchsafe sweet Saint, my Patronesse to bee
To praye for him who humblye prayes to thee

To thee which being borne of Royall blood
Hating the world as . . . at thy owne will,
Lifte all to follow God true Soveraigne Good
who onelye able was thy Soule to fill
Daunting the worlde, the flesh, the feind and Sin.
for Liffe well led, an endless life to win.

For which a Saint thou worthelie art crowned
In heaven above with everlasting bliss
and here on earth belowe likewise renowned
where to thy name a Church erected is
Even there where thou thy life didst lead and leave
And where I with true life did first receive.

For in that Church a Christian I became
And of Christs Church a Member first to bee
And also was Confirmed in the same
for which I thank my god and praye to thee
The work to further in thy Church begun
with prayers that I my race may rightly Run.

H

To

Nicholas Roscarrock's *Life of St Endelien*

En:

To ~~emulate~~ imitate in part thy vertues rare
Thy faith, Hope, Charitie, thy humble mynde
Thy Chastitie, meekness, & thy dyet spare,
And that wch in this worlde is hard to finde
The love wch thou to enimye dedst showe
Reviving him who sought thy overthrowe. /

Unto the three and one, praie thou for this
And all thy fellow Saints wth mee request
That I maye shun to sin and doe amiss
Bewaile sinns past & followe Gods behest
Graunt mee this Grace good God whose might is moste
Thine Blessed ffather, Sonn, & Holighoste. /

There were two wells, wch bare her name, in the forementioned Parish, the one som=
what more distant from the Church then the other, wch hath bene (as it seames) founde out
of late, for more convenience to serve the Church; but that wch is more remote, is said to be
frequented by her in her life time. Her Tombe was defaced in king Henrie the 8 time
and afterwards placed uppon one Mr Hatten in Chandutes, [illegible] being the South side of the
Church, where it standeth at this present, & seameth to have bene verie Auncient; The table
where of is of a Pollished stone like black Marble. / Reed St Eadelme. /

of St Eneda

Saint Eneda was likewise one of St Brechanus Children, as appeareth by the life of St
Necton, Sister to him, St Endelient, St Menevrie, St Mabin & the rest; & hath a Church
dedicated unto her in Cornewalle, where the ffeast is kept ever the first wednesdaye in
March. And yet I finde not so much as the name of this Saint in anie Welsh Pedegree. that I
Reed St Brechanus and St Necton. / I take it [illegible]

of St Englad Bishop & Confessor. /

Saint Englad Bishop and Confessor, who lived in Scotland under king Kenred. an: 366 Novemb: 3.
and hath a ffeast November 3. Callend: Scot: & Buplised by Adame Kinge,

of St Englemund

Saint Englemund whom Molanus calleth Inglemund, was borne of Noble Parentage in Febr: 1.
England, & descended of the Stock of ffreizland, who being a Preist and going to win soules, Jun 21.
became an Abbott of the Order of St Bennet, in the time of St Willibroad, and [illegible]
wth a heavenlie instinct into Holland, where hee Preached the word of God to ffreeze and un=
=tamed Benemarians. And after manie of his holie labours, falling sick of a ffeaver, hee anno 727
yeilded upp his Soule into the handes of our Saviour, & was honorablie buried in the village
of Velsen; where also by his prayers hee caused water to flowe out of the earth. And [illegible]
[illegible] thought his blessed bodie was through the [illegible] found out by
Walderic or Balderic the 2th Bish: of Utricht in the yeare [illegible] his ffeast in the Auncient Mysals
is the first of ffebruarie; but as [illegible] it hath bene celebrated in Sommer
on the 21 of June, on wch daye perhaps hee was Elevated. This Velsen is a Countrie village
of the North of Harlem, where St Englemund saith Molanus in my memorie was renowned
for Miracles, & for his Patronage against the tooth ache; but his Head being sett in golde, &
stolen awaye manie yeres past; the rest of his Relicks were cast or scattred abroad in the fleeld
by the Gueses; but gathered upp by the keper, were secretlie reserved, & are still preserved at Harlem
because all the Houses almost of Velsen, together wth the [illegible] of the Church were
broken downe, burnt, or defaced, partlie by the incursion of the enemye, partlie by the kings Soldiers
to serve

S in the Cambridge University Library)

Bishop Walter Frere with the Prebendaries at the time of the rehabilitation

Bishop Graham Leonard with his Chaplain, Canon Miles Brown, Canon Prest, The Reverend E.C.B. Dunford and the author at the time of the latter's Installation

each other. Only on Saturdays and Sundays did the whole community worship together in church when even the aged Paphnutius was present. They observed a corporate rule concerning sleep, meals and work. Their attitude to poverty and possessions made them reluctant even to have books but these were nevertheless kept, read and written. The writings of Clement and Origen, for example, circulated among the monks. A disciple of Origen was Evagrius whose own writings, written in Greek before 400, aimed at aiding the monks to practise the contemplative life as did those of Cassian, who wrote in Latin between 420 and 430, to whom reference has already been made. The Egyptian monks were, on the whole, simple men who were aware of a tension between simplicity and learning.

The monastic culture and spirituality from St Benedict to St Bernard, about which Jean Leclercq has written so eloquently,[10] was to come later and it is the earlier monasticism of the East from which Celtic monasticism originated.

Mention has been made in the essay on 'The Family of St Endelienta, V.' of the contact between the north-western Celtic lands and the Gallic, Spanish and Mediterranean world. The early monasticism of the East may have reached Cornwall, with which we are chiefly concerned, by a circuitous route. When we recall the presence of Cassian at Marseilles, of Martin in Gaul, of Priscillian in Spain and of Honoratus at Lerins off the coast of Provence we can form some idea of the possible ways in which the monasticism of the desert reached the Cornish Peninsular either directly or via Ireland and/or Wales.

Wherever the monasticism of the East was adopted it was doubtless also adapted by those converted to the religious life but basically that way of life would have been similar to that from which it originated.

Bearing in mind the way of life of the monks of the desert we are now in a position to picture the sort of life which St Endelienta led. One might say that she led the life of a semi-coenobite observing a simple rule of prayer and silence in her cell from which she emerged for corporate worship with

[10] *The Love of Learning* and *the Desire for God–A Study of Monastic Culture;* by Jean Leclercq , O.S.B. SPCK (1978).

other semi-coenobites in the neighbourhood among whom would have been her sister, St Teath, and from which she emerged to proclaim her Christian Faith. In the Age of the Saints the Christian Faith was disseminated by Celtic missionaries among whom there were obviously groups, the Children of Brychan for example, who observed a corporate rule of life whilst living in separate cells set apart from each other but in the same vicinity.

In Cornwall such groups were to be found near the Camel estuary and near the Fowey and Looe estuaries. One might almost consider the cells of the Children of Brychan in these three centres as mission stations. In addition, of course, there were a number of Cornish saints whose love of solitude, like that of Paphnutius in the Egyptian desert, would have taken them to remote places and who, unlike Paphnutius, would not even have joined other Celtic monk-missionaries for corporate worship. St Piran, in his lonely oratory among the sand-dunes, may have been among the latter.

As Celtic Christianity took root and places of worship and priests were provided for the communities of converts it is not unlikely that small communities of priests or seculars, as distinct from monks and nuns, would have become attached to such centres of worship including those founded by the semi-coenobites. These seculars, observing a simple rule and living either together or in separate dwellings, formed communities which might well be considered the genesis of the collegiate system which appeared before the Norman Conquest and proliferated during the centuries which followed it.

St Endelienta's Foundation

The first mention of Ecclesia Sancte Endeliente occurs in the Episcopal Registers of Walter Bronescombe[1] and the date is 1260, several centuries after the Saint's death.

During these centuries the missionary work of such semi-coenobite Celtic saints as St Endelienta and her sister, St Teath, might well have been continued, as has been suggested in the previous essay, by small communities of priests or seculars. Dr Walter Frere, in his address on the occasion of the rehabilitation or reincorporation of St Endelienta's Foundation, spoke of those working in the vicinity of the scene of St Endelienta's labours as "a little colony of Christian priests united in a ministry, perhaps better described as something part-way between a clergy-house and a religious order".

The Celtic Church in the Cornish Peninsular whilst maintaining its contacts with Ireland, Brittany and Wales would seem to have isolated itself for some centuries from the influence of the Christianity of the early English. Its attitude was in line with that of the Celtic Church in other parts of the land. The refusal of the British bishops to assist Augustine in the conversion of the English (by a curious coincidence St Columba, the greatest of the Celtic saints, died in Iona in 597, so it is said, which was the year in which Augustine reached Kent) is attested by the fact that "not one Cumbrian, Welsh, or Cornish missionary to any non-Celtic nation is mentioned anywhere".[2]

The Celtic Church is Northumbria officially abandoned the Celtic for the Roman Order at the Synod of Whitby (663), that in Northern Ireland by the end of the century, that in North Wales by the mid-eighth century, that in South Wales perhaps later still but it was not until the tenth century that Devon and

[1] He was Bishop of Exeter from 1258 to 1280. He commenced the Registers, collected and revised the cathedral statutes and confirmed previous charters. An indefatigable prelate, he consecrated 40 churches in Devon and Cornwall in one year (1268).

[2] Haddan & Stubbs, Councils, i. 154.

Cornwall submitted. The submission of the British bishop Conan to Archbishop Wulfstan enabled Aethelstan, who had conquered Cornwall, to nominate Conan to the see of Bodmin in 936. Nevertheless, evidence that the English element had already been spreading in the Cornish Church comes from English dedications and the appearance of "stowes" and "weeks" in the names of places. It is possible that Alfred (849–99), King of the West Saxons, who possessed property in Triconshire or Trigg (as indicated by his will: Kemble Cod.Diplom. No.314), also paved the way for this submission by placing the spiritual oversight of Trigg in the hands of his chaplain, the Welsh priest Asser, who afterwards became Bishop of Sherborne.

The "little colony of Christian priests united in a ministry, perhaps better described as something part-way between a clergy-house and a religious order" at St Endellion would have been maintained over the centuries[3] but it is significant that St Endellion is not mentioned as landowning or as a quasi-monastic church in the Domesday Book (1086) which notes the monastic or collegiate character of such pre-conquest foundations as St German's Priory and St Buryan's Collegiate Church. The first mention of Ecclesia Sancte Endeliente in 1260, however, is very soon followed by the mention in Bishop Bronescombe's Register of two prebendal appointments. On the Vigil of the Feast of St Catherine 1265/6 Sir Paganus de Liskerret was instituted to that portion of Ecclesia Sancte Endeliente which had previously been held by Richard de Henmerdon. The patron of this prebend was Roger de Bodrugan. Later it was to be called Marny's Prebend because from 1452, or perhaps between 1393 and 1414,[4] until 1524, or

[3] This continued existence, of which we have no evidence that can be compared with that of the similar colonies of missionaries in the North whose monastic settlements resulted in the foundation of the Minsters of Ripon and Beverley (see below), may be asserted because the events which took place in the latter part of the thirteenth century at St Endellion could only have taken place if some form of community life had already been in existence there.

[4] Robert Sympson was presented by Sir John Marny in 1452. John Cergeaux was presented in 1391 by Richard Cergeaux who died in 1393. Henry Shyrston, who succeeded John Cergeaux, may have been presented by Sir William Marny who died in 1414.

perhaps between 1524 and 1558,[5] the patrons were members of the family of that name. On the Saturday next after the Feast of St Lucy 1266 the Bishop made John Bloyou Sub-deacon and instituted him to a portion of Ecclesia Sancte Endeliente. The patron of this prebend (Trehaverock Prebend as it later came to be called) was Robert Modret.

The late Charles Henderson wrote: "The Church of Endellion first appears in 1260 and in 1268 was collegiate, consisting of four Prebendaries. One of the Prebends with the cure of souls attached became entitled the Rectory."[6] Had this great scholar lived to produce his projected survey of all the ecclesiastical foundations in Cornwall he would have amplified this statement and answered the questions it prompts us to ask and which some attempt must be made to answer. I venture to suggest that we should consider why Ecclesia Sancte Endeliente became "collegiate" in 1268 and not before, in what sense it may be considered collegiate vis-à-vis a church of portioners and what was the nature of the corporate life and work of the early portioners or prebends and their successors.

Why was the "collegiate" foundation of Ecclesia Sancte Endeliente post-Conquest (1268) and not pre-Conquest? We have postulated that the missionary work inaugurated by our semi-coenobite Celtic saint, Endelienta, was continued over the centuries by a colony of priests united in a ministry which may be compared with that of similar colonies of missionaries in the North. In the Diocese of York the Minsters of Ripon and Beverley would seem to have derived their origin from Celtic monk missionaries whose settlements provided sites for outposts of missionary work in a large diocese during the seventh and eighth centuries. Their constitution before the Conquest may well have been influenced by the rule of life introduced amongst the priests attached to the cathedral church of Metz by their bishop, Chrodegang of Metz (746–66). This rule of life or canon, adopted elsewhere by communities of secular priests, meant that those who observed it were given the title,

[5] Edmund Benyfeld was Prebend of Marny's in 1537. We do not know the date of his presentation but it may have been made by a member of the Marny family. Viscount Bindon is mentioned as patron for the first time in 1558.

[6] The *Cornish Church Guide.*

in due course, of canons. These secular canons must be distinguished from Regular Canons who were members of the Augustinian Order of Regular Canons[7] and who were priests who had taken monastic vows. Many communities of secular priests were, after the Conquest, converted into houses of Augustinian Canons. The Minsters of Ripon and Beverley were of great importance because they were pre-Conquest collegiate churches, corporate bodies with the obligation to recite the canonical hours and to minister to the spiritual needs of the local congregation and those who lived on the lands with which the foundations were endowed. Because they were situated in Yorkshire, in which county, at the Synod of Whitby (663), the Celtic Church of the North had submitted to the Roman Order, their pre-Conquest origin is likely to have been influenced by Bishop Chrodegang of Metz during the eighth century.

There were, of course, pre-Conquest collegiate foundations in the Diocese of Exeter. Mention has been made of that at St Buryan. The Collegiate Church of Crediton, having a Precentor as its head, reminds us of the period when Crediton was the see of the Bishop of Devon prior to 1050 when Leofric moved his see to Exeter. The Collegiate Churches at St Neot, St Crantock and St Probus can claim to have been founded before the Norman Conquest. As it was not until the tenth century that Devon and Cornwall abandoned the Celtic for the Roman Order, it is unlikely that the pre-Conquest foundations in the Western Peninsular absorbed the rule of life introduced by Bishop Chrodegang of Metz.

Rules of life they undoubtedly observed but these would have been inspired by the disciplined lives of the Celtic missionary saints. This would have been the case at the small colony working in the vicinity of St Endelienta's shrine which based its rule of life upon that of the saint.

At this stage in our search for the reason why Ecclesia Sancte Endeliente became a "collegiate" foundation in 1268 it may be helpful to note the geographical position of the colony at work

[7] Their rule was based largely on the writings of St Augustine of Hippo. See *The Origin of the Austin Canons and Their Introduction into England*, by J. Dickinson.

in the vicinity of St Endelienta's shrine in relation to St Petroc's Priory of Augustinian Canons at Bodmin.

This was founded *c.* 1124[8] by William Warelwast, Bishop of Exeter (1107–38) or, at least, through his instrumentality. The late Canon Taylor cautiously suggested that the Bishop may have given St Endelienta's Church to Bodmin Priory and procured the endowment of the prebends there. It was not until 1272, however, that we have evidence that the Prior and Convent of Bodmin possessed the moiety of St Endelienta's Church. Bishop Walter Bronescombe's Register (folio 51) informs us that in November of that year "Prior et Conventus Bodmin ecclesie Sancte Endeliane medietatis sunt veri patroni". This moiety would seem to have consisted of two portions one of which became the Rectory and the other the Prebend of Bodmin. The remaining two prebends had lay patrons.

The Priory presented William de Tregev, Deacon in 1273. He was the second of the six portioners mentioned in the Episcopal Registers before William Langston who was the first portioner to be given the title of Rector.[9] William de Tregev's predecessor, John de Winton, may also have been presented by the Priory but if this were so his tenure of office would have been of short duration. The Priory also presented William de Doune to the "Bodmin Prebend" in 1342 and it is highly probable that it also presented his three predecessors, Henry de Monketon (1294), William de Monketon (1314) and John de Bos.

I venture to suggest that this close connection between Bodmin Priory and Ecclesia Sancte Endeliente came into being through the instrumentality of Bishop Walter Bronescombe.

This notable prelate had been trained in the royal service and even after his appointment as Bishop of Exeter in 1258 we find him heading the list of twelve bishops and barons appointed after the Battle of Evesham in 1265. Nevertheless, he had settled down to become an assiduous diocesan who was

[8] Charles Henderson (*Essays in Cornish History*, pp. 220–1) says that it was perhaps about the time Algar became Bishop of Countances (?1132).

[9] PRO ms "parson of the Church of Sancta Endelient" in September 1358 (PRO/Just 1/124, m.4)

diligent in visiting the parishes and religious communities in Devon and Cornwall.

On one of his progresses through his diocese he would doubtless have visited Bodmin Priory and have taken an interest in such quasi-monastic settlements as that which had long been in existence at St Endellion. His collection and revision of his cathedral's statutes and his confirmation of previous charters is evidence of his interest in the past and his commencement of Episcopal Registers is evidence of his efficiency.

In the year 1268, during which he consecrated no less than 40 churches in Devon and Cornwall, it is not beyond the bounds of possibility that he would have wished to consolidate the missionary work begun by St Endelienta and continued over the centuries by giving that "little colony of Christian priests united in a ministry, perhaps better described as something part-way between a clergy-house and a religious order" the status of a collegiate body and to associate it with St Petroc's Priory of Augustinian Canons at Bodmin.

The reference to Chaplains among the Rectors of St Endellion and among the Bodmin Prebends is evidence that the Augustinian Rule precluded members of the community at Bodmin Priory from performing pastoral work themselves and the Priory was not overzealous for the spiritual well-being of the parishioners of St Endellion. The work of Bishop Bronescombe's collegiate foundation was maintained nevertheless from 1268 onwards.

In what sense was St Endelienta's Foundation a collegiate church vis-à-vis a church of portioners? It is difficult to distinguish between genuine collegiate foundations and churches of portioners. The latter were churches with revenues divided among a number of portioners, usually four or three. These churches resembled those rectories, common throughout the land, which were divided into moieties which were due to the existence of two patrons or the division of the inheritance of one patron. Tiverton and Chumleigh in Devon and St Endellion, St Probus and St Teath in Cornwall have been considered as such by some scholars. It has been pointed out that although such churches have often been treated as collegiate they nevertheless possessed none of the corporate signs of a college. They had no common seal nor fund, no chapter meetings were held and each portioner was a corporation sole.[10] The Episcopal Registers of the Diocese of Hereford provide us with evidence of a test case. In 1384 the Bishop, John Gilbert, ordered an enquiry into the status of the churches of Ledbury and Bromyard. The jurors pronounced them to be churches of portioners as neither had dean or master, common seal or buildings, chest or chapter-house.

We can, however, assert that St Endelienta's Foundation was a collegiate church. At a Provincial Council or Synod held in 1341 the "Canons" of Endellion signed as the "Chapter of St Endelienta". Just as the Collegiate Church of St Thomas, Glasney had a Provost, that of Crediton, a Precentor and that of Westbury-on-Trym a Dean so St Endellion had a Rector (*c.* 1358). Although the members of the College of St Endellion did not inhabit a common residence the Prebendal Houses were in close proximity.[11] The absence of original statutes or a common seal is regrettable but if we have no evidence of the existence of them we may assume that they were lost along with other documents relating to the Foundation.

This loss of documents makes it well-nigh impossible to envisage the nature of the corporate life and work of the early portioners or prebends. We can only assume that they carried out their pastoral and collegiate duties aided by the prayers of their patroness. Of their deficiencies, which we must also assume, we may seek for enlightenment by noting an account, of which we have evidence, of the visitation of the Collegiate Church of Rouen by Archbishop Odo of Rigaud in November

[10] "A prebendary has two capacities, sole and aggregate: for he is a member of a corporation aggregate, and has a sole capacity in respect of his fellowship" (Ayliffe, *State of the University of Oxford*, vol.ii, p.23), cf. "A canon is, by himself, a corporation sole. He is also a member of the corporation aggregate, namely, the corporation of the dean and chapter" (Halsbury's *Laws of England*, Pt II, Section 6 iv 256, p.120) "In some chapters the canons were formerly known as prebendaries" (ibid). "A prebend was formerly described as an endowment in land, or pension in money given to a cathedral or conventual church in praebendam, that is, for the maintenance of a secular priest or regular canon who was a prebendary..."(ibid.).

[11] Just as the Provost of Worcester, the Dean of Christ Church or the Rector of Exeter College, Oxford lived in close proximity to the fellows of these foundations.

1266.[12] This visitation informs us "... that the canons and choir clerks talk and chatter from stall to stall, and across each other, while the divine office is being celebrated. They hasten through the psalms too quickly. The chaplains celebrate the mass inadequately...". Of one priest it was reported that "He did not have the letters of his ordination; he could not tell by whom or through whom he had been ordained; he was also ill-famed of trading...". The report ends "then we asked the chapter for our procuration (expenses) by reason of the aforesaid visitation".

Such shortcomings in the Collegiate Church of Rouen would not be unknown in other colleges and in parish churches on both sides of the Channel in the thirteenth century. In 1248 Archibishop Odo visited the Deanery of Brachi near St Just in Normandy. We learn that the Chaplain of Brachi frequented taverns, that Simon, the Priest of St Just was pugnacious and quarrelsome and that the Priest of Dufranville does not stay there and goes to England without permission.

Before leaving the early years of the Collegiate Church of St Endelienta we can take note of the composition of the Chapter of the College towards the end of the thirteenth century. The Taxatio (taxation of benefices) made by the Bishops of Lincoln and Winchester (Oliver Sutton and John of Pontoise) in 1291[13] records four prebends or portions:

Prebenda Domini Pagani de Liskerit (Sir Paganus de Liskerit) Taxation £3 Tenths s.6 0	The portion later called Marny's
Prebenda Johannis de Moderet (John Modret) Taxation £3 Tenths s.6 0	The portion later called Trehaverock
Prebenda Henrici de Moncatone (Henry de Monketon) Taxation £4.2s Tenths s.8 2	The portion called Bodmin
Prebenda Domini Reginaldi (Sir Reginald de Karentoc) Taxation £4.2s Tenths s.8 2	Portioner of St Endellion

[12] *Regestrum visitationum archiepiscopi Rothomagensis.*

[13] Sir John Maclean says 1294 and Charles Henderson 1288. The Taxatio was somewhat

For what is known of these prebends and their successors reference may be made to the essay, "Portioners, Rectors, Prebends and Patrons".

How was it that St Endelienta's thirteenth-century Collegiate Foundation escaped suppression in the sixteenth century? Following the Acts of Parliament (1536: 27 Hen.VIII, c.28; 1539: 31 Hen.VIII, c.13) to dissolve religious houses and augment the King's revenue, the Chantries Act (37 Hen.VIII c.4) was passed in 1545. This was "An Acte for the Dissolution of Colleges, Chantries, and Free Chappells at the King's Majesties Pleasure". Commissions to put this into effect were issued in 1546 but on 28th January 1547 Henry VIII died. With his death went the power to issue commissions but after the brief respite enjoyed by the chantries the work of suppression was inherited by Edward VI on whose behalf a new act for their suppression (1 Ed.VI c.14) was passed in 1547 and a new body of commissioners was appointed to carry it out.

In 1549 the Chantry Commissioners reported that the object of the three prebends of St Endellion, William Cavell (Trehaverock), Edmund Benyfeld (Marny's) and John Parry (Bodmin), was to help in the ministration of Divine Service in the Parish Church. Charles Henderson (MS notes) says: "At the time, one of the prebends, Cavell's or Trehaverock's was a pluralist and non resident; the other two, Marny's and Bodmin had no other benefice and were therefore probably in residence." All three received pensions of £5 (in connection with pensions paid to dispossessed religious) but only Edmund Benyfeld is mentioned as having been deprived (Bp Turberville's Reg. fol.45). No mention is made of John Bere, the Rector, who headed a staff of clergy (see under "Rectors"). The Commissioners would seem charitably to have regarded the prebends as "curates" who were "superannuated". Deo gratias (and thanks to St Endelienta) their successors and that of the Rector were all appointed "prebends" and the prebendal lineage remained unbroken. Neighbouring St Teath was not spared. As we shall now see, in the eighteenth century the

carelessly compiled. It was bitterly resented as were those of 1219 and 1256. A Canon of Barnwell commenting upon them says: "Prima pungit, secunda vulnerat, tercia usque ad ossa excoriat".

Rector and prebends are noted with their patrons but of St Teath is noted "olim a College".

The following extract from a copy of the Valor Ecclesiasticus of Henry VIII published in 1786[14] (apropos Queen Anne's Bounty, a fund formed by Queen Anne in 1704 to receive the first fruits–annates–and tenths which had been confiscated by Henry VIII) is of interest:

[14] LIBER REGIS DEL THESAURUS RERUM ECCLESIASTICARUM by John Bacon, Esq. Receiver of the First Fruits. London, printed for the author by John Nichols MDCCLXXXVI.

D. Trigge Minor
Livings Remaining in Charge

Rectories, &c, with their Patrons, Proprietors, &c.

King's Books l.	s.	d.		Yearly Tenths l.	s.	d.
10	0	0	St Endelian R. Omn. decim. Syn. & Prox. 2s. 2d½ The	1	0	0
100	0	0	KING			
5	0	0	Heredum Marny, alias Mornays in Endelian Church, P. Syn. & Prox. 2s. 2d.½ Earl of Radnor, 1716, 1738. George Hunt,Esq.1777	0	10	0
5	0	0	Prioris Bodmyn P. alias King's Preb. Syn. 2s. 2d.½ Serj. Jo. Belfield, this Turn, 1712. Francis Bassett, Esq. 1779,	0	10	0
12	0	0	St. Tethe V. olim a College. Decim. major. & minor. Syn. 8s. 9d. Bishop of Exeter, p.i.	1	4	0
5	0	0	Trehaverock P. in Endelian. Syn. 2s. 2d.½ Richardson Grey, and Catherine Grey, 1718. John Gray, 1733. Catherine Dagge, 1754. Thomas Gray, Gent. 1784	0	10	0

Chapels, Donatives, and Curacies

Lanhedwick, alias Lanhidrock, Cur. (St. Hydrock.) Pri Bodmyn, Propr. This Curacy has no Endowment; but the Prebend of Heredam Marny being in the same Patronage, is usually given to the Curate of Lanhidrock. George Hunt, Esq.

The Prebendal Almuce

The fur cape and hood worn by the Prebendaries of the Collegiate Church of St Endelienta is called an almuce (almucium, aumuce, amess), a medieval vestment the history of which is of interest.

It would seem that it appeared in the thirteenth century (when it was simply a strip of fur) and that from the fourteenth to the sixteenth centuries it took the shape of that reproduced for the Prebendaries of St Endellion at the time of the rehabilitation of the collegiate foundation.

Its original purpose would seem to have been practical–to keep its wearer warm during the recitation of the Divine Office in Choir. There is an effigy of a Canon of Sainte-Marie at Noyon, who died in 1353, which depicts him wearing an almuce of black cloth lined with white material (fluffy cotton or silk) the hood of which was padded since the wearer may well have rested his head against the carvings of his stall.

Originally introduced as a concession to comfort it became an emblem of dignity. Dignitaries would wear an almuce lined with fur (squirrel, sable or even ermine) and eventually the fur lining was displayed by being used as the material for the outside of the almuce. At the same time the ordinary black cloth (formerly used for the outside of the almuce) was discarded and the new lining was of some colourful and rich fabric. Another innovation was the provision of long stole-like ends of fur depending from the front of the almuce.

A brass in Exeter Cathedral depicts Canon William Langeton wearing such a fur almuce beneath a cope (1413) and the brass of Thomas Teylor (*c.* 1480) who was Rector of Byfleet, Surrey shows him, as a Canon of Lincoln, vested in a white fur almuce. The brass of John Mapilton (1432) at Broadwater, Sussex depicts him in the processional vestments of surplice, almuce and cope. Documentary evidence is provided by a Lichfield Cathedral Statute (1420–47)[1] which laid down that the

[1] Dugdale: *Monasticon* VI iii p. 1263.

succentor, as well as the dean, chancellor and treasurer, should wear an almuce trimmed with calabar fur.

The almuce continued to be worn in England up to the sixteenth century. At the Obsequy for Henry II of France at St Paul's, 8th and 9th September, 1559,[2] mention is made of two prebendaries in their gray amices (almuces) and at a Procession at Windsor on St George's Day, 18th May 1561, reference is made to the wearing of gray ames (almuces) in calabur.[3] In the following year Archbishop Parker and his suffragans wore amess and habit at Convocation, 13th January.[4]

It would seem that up to the reign of Edward VI the choir habit in cathedral and collegiate churches consisted of a surplice or rochet, an amess (for the upper and middle ranks), and a black cloth cope or cloak, called a cappa nigra. In about the year 1566, however, although at the beginning of the reign of Elizabeth I (1558) canons wore fur amesses, there is to be found a curious reference to "Grosse pointes of Poperie, evident unto all men ... Silken hoodes in their quiers, upon a surplesse. The gray amise with cattes tayles"[5] and, a few years later, the Canons of 1571 require that: "No Deane, nor Archdeacon, nor Residentarie, nor Master, nor Warden, nor head of any college, or cathedrall churche, neither President, nor Rector, nor any of yt order, by what name soeuer they be called, shall hereafter weare the Graye Amice (almuce)."'[6]

About two years later (*c.* 1573) a comment on the Canons of 1571 includes a reference to the almuce: "We marvel that they could espy in their last Synod, that a gray amice, which is but a garment of dignity, should be a garment (as they say) defiled with superstition, and yet that copes, caps, surplices, tippets, and suchlike baggage, the preaching signs of popish priesthood, the Pope's creatures, kept in the same form to this end to bring dignity and reverence to the ministers and sacraments, should be retained still, and not abolished."[7]

[2] Strype's *Annals*, I.i.189.

[3] *Diary of Henry Machyn*, p.258. Camden Society, 1848.

[4] Cardwell: *Synodalia*, ii. 497, 498.

[5] Quoted in the *British Magazine* xxi 625.

[6] Cardwell: *Synodalia*, i. 115, 116.

[7] *A View of Popish Abuses yet Remaining in the English Church*, p.17.

The almuce which was "but a garment of dignity" was abolished in England in 1571 but with the rehabilitation of the Collegiate Church of St Endelienta in 1929 it was restored and splendidly reproduced for the use of the Prebendaries of that ancient foundation. They enjoy what must be a unique privilege in the Anglican Church.

Portioners, Rectors, Prebends and Patrons from the Thirteenth to the Mid-nineteenth Centuries

Apart from names and dates and, in some cases, a few biographical details we know very little about the Portioners, Rectors, and Prebends of St Endelienta's Foundation. None of them achieved the sort of fame which would merit their inclusion in the *Dictionary of National Biography*. Most of them were born and bred in Cornwall. Some of them were educated at a university and it is not surprising that most of these matriculated at Exeter College, Oxford, founded by a West Country Bishop, Walter de Stapeldon, and therefore considered to be a West Country college.

Pluralism was not unknown among them and during the eighteenth century three Rectors in succession were also Prebends of Trehaverock. The majority of them died in office and few resigned. Those deprived and the sole case of recusancy have been noted in a previous essay. By and large, they were typical of parish priests generally in the times in which they lived.

The following lists give such details as we have of the Portioners and Rectors as fully as possible. Of the three other prebends that of Marny's sets out the wording of the appointment in some detail as a matter of interest but, for the sake of space, those of the other two prebends in less detail.

The history of the patrons is outside the scope of these essays with the exception of the Prior and Convent of Bodmin to which reference has been made in a previous essay. For information about the families of the other patrons the works of Sir John Maclean, C.S. Gilbert and Lake are of course invaluable.

Master John de Winton **No date**

Nothing is known of him. His tenure and death are mentioned in the records concerning his successors.

William de Tregev, Deacon **1273**

The Bishop committed to him the moiety of the Church of Endellion (vacant by the death of Master John de Winton) to which he was presented by the Prior and Convent of Bodmin. (Bishop Bronescombe's Register folio 51.)

Master Thomas de Bocland **6th January 1275–6**

The Bishop conveyed to him the portion (formerly held by John de Winton) together with the cure of souls. It was in the gift of the Bishop by lapse. No mention is made of the death of William de Treger. (Bishop Bronescombe's Register folio 59a.)

Sir Reginald de Karentoc, Priest **April 1278**

He was collated to the portion held by John de Winton "so long vacant". No mention is made of the death of Thomas de Bocland. Had the latter's tenure slipped the scribe's mind? Karentoc was Crantock. The College there was founded *c.* 1236. (Bishop Bronescombe's Register folio 60d.)

Master Thomas de Polhorman **1308**

Bishop Stapeldon's Register (folio 37b) records that Thomas de Polhorman was granted a licence of non-residence for the purpose of study. Polhorman was a manor which lay partly in Tywardreth. One wonders if Master Thomas pursued his studies at the Benedictine Priory there.

Master Richard de St Margaret **2nd April 1312**

He was collated to the portion held by Thomas de Polhorman by the Bishop because of the default of the Prior and Convent of Bodmin. (Bishop Stapeldon's Register folio 71.)

William Langston **c.1358**

His tenure and death are mentioned in the records concerning his successor. We learn from another source (Public Records Office/Just 1/124, m.4) that William Langstone was "parson of the Church of Sancta Endelient" in September 1358.

Stephen de Longeney, Priest **13th January 1376**

He was collated to the Parish Church of Endellion, vacant by the death of William Langston, in the collation of the Bishop by lapse. (Bishop Brentingham's Reg. fol. 46.)

Walter Typet **No date**

His tenure and death are mentioned in the records concerning his successor.

Nicholas Langston, Priest **5th July 1377**

He was instituted to the Parish Church of Endellion, vacant by the death of Walter Typet, upon presentation by the Prior and Convent of Bodmin. (Bishop Brentingham's Reg. fol. 50.)

Roger Masek **No date**

His tenure and death are mentioned in the records concerning his successor.

John Henry, Chaplain **20th March 1394**

He was instituted to the Church of St Endellion, vacant by the death of Roger Masek, upon presentation by the Prior and Convent of Bodmin. (Bishop Stafford's Reg. fol. 26.)

The Register of Exeter College, Oxford has an entry for John Henry/Herry/Harry of Cornwall. He was in residence: Summer 1372 to Winter 1379; M.A., Vice-Rector 1377–8. Afterwards he would seem to have been a somewhat peripatetic priest. He was Vicar of Gwennap (1381) and Rector of Endellion (1394). The Register then says that he exchanged benefices with the

Vicar of Gwinear (1404/5) from which living he resigned in 1438. I venture to suggest that for Gwinear we should read Winnow. As we shall see, his successor at St Endellion, Thomas Berty, had been Vicar of St Winnow. The Register of Exeter College, Oxford also records that a licence was given to John Harry, Vicar of Wynner on 10th October 1411 (Stafford's Reg. 117, 123, 141) to celebrate in a chapel of St Wynner. If this refers, as I am of the opinion that it does, to the chapel dedicated to St Nectan in the parish of St Winnow, then it is more than likely that a former Rector of the Parish of St Endelienta would wish to celebrate in a chapel dedicated to her brother.

Thomas Berty **19th March 1405**

Formerly Vicar of St Winnow, he was instituted to the Rectory of St Endellion by exchange with John Harry/Henry and upon presentation by (or, one might say, with the permission of) the Prior and Convent of Bodmin. (Bishop Stafford's Reg. fol. 83.)

John Worthyn **28th October 1410**

Formerly Rector of Farendon, he was instituted Rector of St Endellion upon exchange with Thomas Berty and with the consent of the Patron, the Prior and Convent of Bodmin. (Bishop Stafford's Reg. fol. 129.)

John Wolston, Clerk **6th April 1414**

He was collated to the Church of Endellion, the right of collation having devolved upon the Bishop. (Bishop Stafford's Reg. fol. 158.)

William Gorteboos, Clerk **13th July 1416**

He was instituted to the Church of St Endellion upon presentation by the Prior and Convent of Bodmin. (Bishop Stafford's Reg. fol. 178.)

John Talwargh **No date**

His tenure and resignation are mentioned in the records concerning his successor.

John Harry, Chaplain **5th May 1435**

He was instituted to the Parochial Church of St Endellion, vacant by the resignation of John Talwargh, upon presentation by the Prior and Convent of Bodmin. (Bishop Lacy's Reg. Vol.II fol. 135.)

William Harry, Clerk **18th December 1441**

Filling the vacancy caused by the resignation of John Harry, he was instituted upon presentation by the Prior and Convent of Bodmin. (Bishop Lacy's Reg. Vol.II fol. 196.)

One wonders if William Harry's tenure was later a sinecure. The Bishop's Register (Vol.II fol. 355) records that on 11th December 1450 letters compulsory were issued by William Harry, Rector, to compel John Cutbert, the Chaplain celebrating at Bodmin, but without cure of souls, to serve the cure at St Endellion for a competent salary. Process was issued to Sir John Lovebounde, Chaplain, to move him to admit John Cutbert to the cure aforesaid: and if he, the said John, should not yield obedience to these instructions, that then he should be cited before the Bishop, or his Commissary, on the twelfth day after the citation to shew reasonable cause, or causes, why he should not be suspended from his office, or from the celebration of Divine Service. It is evidence that pressure could be brought to bear in dealing with such matters.

John Graddon **22nd January 1454**

Filling the vacancy caused by the death of William Harry, he was instituted upon presentation by the Prior and Convent of Bodmin. (Bishop Lacy's Reg. Vol.II fol. 286.) Two Inquisitions dated 1444 and 1445 mention William Hutchyn as Rector but Hutchyn would seem to have been a misprint for Harry.

Thomas Rowe, Chaplain **15th September 1457**

Filling the vacancy caused by the resignation of John Graddon, he was instituted upon presentation by the Prior and Convent of Bodmin. (Bishop Nevyll's Reg. fol. 5.)

Henry Gurlyn, Clerk **15th October 1462**

Filling the vacancy caused by the death of Thomas Rowe, he was instituted. It was certified, on 25th September 1462, upon a Commission issued to Henry Webber, Dean of Exeter, that Thomas the Prior, and the Convent of Bodmin are the true patrons, and that William Vyvyan, the late Prior, made the last presentation. (Bishop Nevyll's Reg. fol. 24 & 86.) Gurlyn was also Vicar of Bodmin and died in 1470.

Stephen Luky, Chaplain **7th June 1469**

Filling the vacancy caused by Henry Gurlyn, he was instituted upon presentation by the Prior and Convent of Bodmin. (Bishop Bothe's Reg. fol. 15.)

Stephen Edward **No date**

His tenure and death are mentioned in the records concerning his successor.

Thomas Buttlar, Chaplain **31st July 1501**

Filling the vacancy caused by the death of Stephen Edward, he was instituted upon presentation by the Prior and Convent of Bodmin. (Bishop Redman's Reg. fol. 22.) On 23rd November 1499 the Bishop granted to Sir Thomas Butler licence to treat upon a pension with Sir John Ruby. (Bishop Oldham's Reg. fol. 14.)

John Ruby **24th May 1508**

Filling the vacancy caused by the resignation of Thomas Butler/Buttlar, he was instituted upon presentation by the Prior and Convent of Bodmin. (Bishop Oldham's Reg. fol. 18.)

William Kingdon/Kyngdon, M.A. **19th May 1533**

Filling the vacancy caused by the death of John Reby/Ruby, he was instituted upon presentation by the Prior and Convent of Bodmin. (Bishop Veysey's Reg. fol. 65.) William Kingdon was admitted to Exeter College, Oxford in 1504, B.A. 1506, M.A. 1509. He was auditor of Rothbury Chest and Guardian of Queen's Chest in 1513. He left the College in 1514.

James Bere (John Bere) **23rd May 1534**

Filling the vacancy caused by the resignation of William Kingdon, he was instituted upon presentation of Richard Roscarroke, by grant from the Prior and Convent of Bodmin, for this turn the true patron. (Bishop Veysey's Reg. fol. 72.) John Bere was in residence at Exeter College, Oxford from 1521 to 1531. He supplicated B.A. (1517) and M.A. (1520) and was in priest's orders by the winter of 1521. He was Rector of the College from 1529 to 1531. The Register of Exeter College records that he was Rector of Endellion 1534, of Camborne 1542 and that he died in 1563. He must have held both livings in plurality for in 1563/4 St Endellion was vacant by his death. He certainly had clerical assistance other than any rendered by the Prebends for in 1537 the emoluments of the staff of St Endellion were as follows:

Master John Bere, Rector	4s
Dom. Robert Kaye, Curate	20d
Dom. David Donell	18d
Master Thomas Brerwood (Bodmin P.)	18d
Master William Cavell (Trehaverock)	18d
Master Edmund Bedyngfyld (Marny's)	18d

John Peryn, Clerk **10th February 1563/4**

Filling the vacancy caused by the death of John Bere, he was instituted by presentation of Robert John of Cardynham for this turn the true patron by the grant of Thomas Wandsworth, Vicar of Bodmin. (Bishop Turberville's Reg. fol. 80; Compounded for First Fruits, 10th February 1564, Augmentation Off.)

Edward Hender/Hendra **12 September 1572**

He was admitted to the Rectory, vacant by the death of the last incumbent, upon presentation by the Queen. (Bishop Bradbridge's Reg. fol. 10.)

Martin Hendra **27th May 1589**

He was instituted to the Rectory, vacant by the death of Edward Hendra, upon presentation by the Queen. (Bishop Babington's Reg. fol. 42; cf. Bishop's Certificates, Augmentation Office.)

Joachin Ball, M.A. **23rd December 1596**

He was admitted to the Rectory, vacant by the death of Martin Hendra, upon presentation by the Queen. (Bishop Babington's Reg. fol. 62.)

Joachim Ball, Clerk **5th July 1597**

He was admitted to the Rectory, vacant by the deprivation of Joachin Ball, ipso facto, because the said Joachin was a recusant, upon presentation by the Queen. (Bishop Babington's Reg. fol. 62.)

It is possible that Joachim Ball and Joachin Ball were one and the same person. Indeed, the first of these gentlemen is named Joachin in the second of the above two entries. The Joachin Ball admitted to the Rectory on 5th July 1597 was succeeded by William Haward on 23rd August 1599 because of a vacancy cuased by the "resignation" of Joachim Beall. The scribe may have presented us with three different spellings of the name of one and the same person. If this is so, then the solution to the mystery would seem to be that a Joachim/Joachin Ball/Beall was a recusant admitted on 23rd December 1596 and deprived either on 5th July 1597 or at some date before 23rd August 1599.

William Haward, Clerk **23rd August 1599**

He was admitted to the Rectory upon presentation by the Queen. (Bishop Carey's Reg. fol. 64.)

Stephen Cavell, Clerk **2nd January 1612**

He was admitted to the Rectory upon presentation by the King. (Bishop Carey's Reg. fol. 100.)

Samuel Rundle/Randle, Clerk **3rd April 1630**

He was admitted to the Rectory, vacant by the death of Stephen Cavell, upon presentation by the King. (Bishop Hall's Reg. fol.19; cf. Bishop's Certs. Aug. Off.) The Register of Exeter College, Oxford, where he matriculated 1619, names him Randall/Rondall and says he was Rector of Bradstone (1622) and of Endellion (1630–60.)

John Wills, Clerk **10th January 1660**

He was admitted to the Rectory, vacant by the death of Samuel Randall, upon presentation by the King. (Bishop Gauden's Reg. fol. 3.) The Register of Exeter College, Oxford, where he matriculated on 28th March 1653, tells us that he was the son of the Reverend John Wills, that he was Rector of Endellion and that he died in 1709.

At a Triennial Visitation held in 1665, John Wills reported that there were three sinecure prebends, two held by John Orchard, Vicar of St Kew and one held by John Snell, Vicar of Lanly. He makes mention of a pastoral matter. He says that "for the benefit of my own son" and also "by the importunity of some of my neighbours I doe spend some houres in instructing them".

From the Cornish Glebe Terriers (1673–1735) we learn that the Rectory *c.* 1679 was "floored with earth" and had the following accommodation: hall, buttery, dairy, kitchen, brew-house, three chambers and a small study. There were two small gardens with a mowhay (*c.* ⅛ acre). Details are given of the Glebe with which we need not be concerned.

John Wills is one of the few former Rectors of whose way of life we can form a faint picture from the few such references given above.

Jonathan Dagge, Clerk, M.A. **26th May 1709**

He was admitted to the Rectory, vacant by the death of the last incumbent, upon presentation by the Queen. (Bishop's Reg. New Series Vol.IV fol.14.) Son of John Dagge of Bodmin, he matriculated as a poor scholar at Christ Church, Oxford on 15th November 1678, B.A. (1682) and M.A. (1685). He was appointed Vicar of Fowey in 1700. He was admitted to the Prebend of Trehaverock on 12th February 1717.

John Dagge, Clerk, M.A. **24th November 1730**

He was admitted to the Rectory, vacant by the resignation of his father, Jonathan Dagge, upon presentation by the King. (Bishop's Reg. New Series Vol.VI fol. 96.) He matriculated at Queen's College, Oxford (11th July 1722).

In 1746 he reported that there were 200 families in the parish of which four were Quakers and that the parish had no school nor Charity. He says that he resided in his Vicarage of Fowey. His father had presumably resigned from this living too in order that his son could enjoy both benefices. John Dagge goes on to mention his presentation to the Rectory of Endellion by Lord Chancellor King and his presentation to the Prebend of Trehaverock by John Gray of Endellion in 1733. He adds that Mr Morrison was presented by John Basset of Yauton in Devon (he was referring to Thomas Morrison's presentation to the Prebend of Bodmin in 1736) and that Mr Daniel Debat was presented by Henry, Earl of Radnor to Marny's (this was in 1738).

He then provides us with some interesting information about the Prebends: "There is no duty lies upon us as Prebends but the Rector or Curate officiates. My curate, Mr Tho. Poulton, is resident with £30 salary. He also serves Tintagel." Finally, he makes a brief reference to public worship in the parish: "Service is performed once a Sunday. There are three celebrations [presumably during the year]. One hundred communicants but only eight at Easter."

Mydhope Wallis, Clerk, B.A. **7th April 1753[1]**

He was admitted to the Rectory, vacant by the death of John Dagge, upon presentation by the King. (Bishop's Reg. New Series Vol.VIII fol. 29.) He matriculated at Balliol College, Oxford (20th May 1735). His curate from 1759 to 1764 was the Reverend W. Buckingham who was commended in 1760 by John Wesley for an excellent sermon delivered by the Curate of Endellion in his presence. It seems that the Reverend W. Buckingham joined John Wesley for two years but then thought better of his action. His temporary defection cost him his curacy at St Endellion. John Wesley, in his *Journal*, reports that on 16th September 1766 he rode to Port Isaac, "now one of the liveliest places in Cornwall". "Here", he says, "Mr Buckingham met me, who, for fear of offending the Bishop, broke off all commerce with the Methodists. He had no sooner done this than the Bishop rewarded him by turning him out of his curacy, which, had he continued to walk in Christian simplicity, he would probably have had to this day."

Thomas Drake, Clerk, M.A. **15th March 1774**

He was admitted to the Rectory, vacant by the cession of Mydhope Wallis, upon presentation by the King. (Bishop's Reg. New Series Vol.IX fol. 97.)

William Spry, Clerk **18th August 1777**

He was admitted to the Rectory, vacant by the cession of Thomas Drake, upon presentation by the King. (Bishop's Reg. New Series Vol.IX fol.134.)

In 1779 he reported that Mr James Evans, the Curate, resides in the Parsonage and that he has a salary of £40. The Rector has no other benefice. He says there are 148 families in the parish. There are some Quakers and Methodists with Meeting Houses.

[1] He was admitted to the Prebend of Trehaverock on the same day.

William Edward Dillon **15th May 1796**

He was admitted to the Rectory, vacant by the death of William Spry, upon presentation by the King. (Bishop's Reg. New Series Vol.X fol.108.)

We have information about the parish during his tenure from the answers he gave to queries put to him by Bishop Carey before a Visitation of the parish. This took place in 1821.

There were about 200 families in the parish but he does not give the number of Methodists. There were Methodist and Quaker Meeting Houses but the latter was seldom if ever used because no Quaker resided in the parish.

William Dillon did not reside in the Rectory "the house not being fit for my family and the state of my wife's health not permitting it". However, he declared that it was "in decent repair for the Curate who resides in it". This licensed curate was Nicholas Tresidder who received £60 per annum.

In addition to St Endellion, he had the cure of souls of Cornelly where he performed Divine Service. At St Endellion Divine Service was performed twice every Lord's Day with a sermon in the morning. The Lord's Supper was administered four times yearly (Christmas, Easter, Whitsuntide and Michaelmas) and there were about twenty communicants. In reply to the questions "Are your church and chancel in good repair?" "Is your churchyard well kept?" and "Have you all things decent for Divine Service?" he was able to say: "All in good order and decent."

There was a Sunday School where the youth of the parish were catechized. There were no benefactions for the church or the poor. Nor were there alms-houses, hospitals, a parish library. There was a Terrier in the Registrar's Office in Exeter.

William Hocken, B.A. **8th October 1833**

He was instituted to the Rectory, vacant by the death of William Dillon, upon presentation by the King. (Bishop's Reg. New Series Vol.XII fol.88.)

He was the son of a blacksmith in the neighbouring parish of St Teath and on one occasion, it is related, he hung a horseshoe over the pulpit and expounded upon its significance prompted by some disparaging reference to his lowly origin.

He was a bright boy and his ability was brought to the notice of Chancellor Lord Brougham who sent him up to Cambridge and, in due course, presented him to the Rectory of St Endellion.

At St Endellion, where he was a good and faithful parish priest, he was regarded by some as a Papist because his visits to the Continent had attracted him to the teaching of the Roman Catholic Church. Indeed, under his influence, his adopted daughter and a local farmer were both received into that Church. He himself remained an Anglican. His foster-daughter gave an account to Canon Carter (Prebend of Bodmin in 1880) of his last days. Whilst the Vicar of St Teath was giving him the Viaticum, the Roman Catholic priest from Liskeard arrived at the Rectory and urged her to allow him to approach William Hocken's death-bed. "He has been a Catholic at heart for many years," he said, "and should be received into the Church." "I shall not let you go up," she replied. "He shall die as he has lived."

Parson Hocken of St Endellion, like Parson Hawker of Morwenstow, was a Cornish character and 'Catholic' parish priest. His hobbies included the cultivation of roses and wheat growing. He introduced a variety of wheat locally named 'purgatory' which may indicate that his Catholic teaching was, at least, listened to.

Marny's Prebend

Richard de Henmerdon **No date**

His tenure is mentioned in the records concerning his successor.

Sir Paganus de Liskerret **Vigil of S.Catherine 1265**

Instituted to that portion lately held by Sir Richard de Henmerdon upon presentation by Roger de Bodrugan. (Bishop Bronescombe's Reg. 28b; the Taxation of the Bishops of Lincoln and Winchester mention that Sir Paganus de Liskerret held the portion in 1294.)

Baldwin de Bello Campo **No date**

His tenure is mentioned in the records concerning his successor. He may have been related to Robert de Bello Campo who founded the Augustinian Priory at Frithelstock *c.* 1220.

Sir Thomas de St Erco **14th May 1340**

Instituted to that portion lately held by Baldwin de Bello Campo upon presentation by Sir William de Bodrugan. (Bishop Grandison's Reg.Vol.III fol.22.)

Thomas de Bodrigan/Bodrugan **23rd April 1349**

Instituted to that portion lately held by Sir Thomas de St Erco upon presentation by Margaret, late wife of Sir Otho de Bodrigan/Bodrugan, deceased, in right of her dower. (Bishop Grandison's Reg.Vol.III fol. 78.)

Richard de Hathelesey, Priest **24th June 1351/7**

Admitted to that portion lately held by Thomas de Bodrigan/ Bodrugan upon presentation by Sir William de Bodrigan/ Bodrugan. (Bishop Grandison's Reg. Vol.III fol. 98.)

Wiliam Cergeaux **No date**

His tenure and death are mentioned in the records concerning his successor. A William Cergeaux is mentioned in 1356. (*Collectanea Cornubiensia*, ed. G.C. Boase, 1890.)

John Cergeaux, Clerk **26th May 1391**

Instituted to the prebend, vacant by the death of William Cergeaux, upon presentation by Sir Richard Cergeaux. (Bishop Brentingham's Reg. fol.122.) The Register of Exeter College, Oxford, lists him as M.A. and a Fellow of the College.

Henry Shyrston **No date**

His tenure and resignation are mentioned below.

Thomas Trevilian, Clerk **8th November 1452**

Instituted, following the resignation of Henry Shyrston, upon presentation by Sir John Marny. (Bishop Lacy's Reg. fol. 272.)

John Millier, Chaplain **22nd August 1466**

Instituted to the prebend, vacant by the death of Thomas Trevilian, upon presentation by Sir John Marny. (Bishop Bothe's Reg. fol. 5.) On 15th June 1466 the Bishop issued a commission to enquire about the patronage. At an Inquisition (held on 10th July at St Mabyn) which noted the death of Thomas Trevilian (3rd March 1465) Sir John Marny was declared the patron by right of inheritance. William Sprigges had been admitted to this Prebend upon presentation of Thomas Younge, Robert Holbeine and John Avery. Before John Millier's institution took place, he resigned in the presence of John Symon, Canon, John Ryse and William Eliot, Registrar. (Bishop Bothe's Reg.) This confirmation of Sir John Marny's patronage against intrusion is of interest. It demonstrates the vigilance and efficiency of episcopal administration at that time.

William Badley, Junior **28th May 1488**

Instituted to the prebend, vacant by the resignation of John Millier, upon presentation by Henry Marny of the County of Essex. (Bishop Bothe's Reg. fol. 103.)

Thomas Ashley, Literate **2nd May 1509**

Instituted to the prebend, vacant by the dismissal of William Badley, upon presentation by Sir William Marny. (Bishop Oldham's Reg. fol. 34.)

Robert Sympson, M.A. **7th March 1524**

Instituted to the prebend, vacant by the death of Thomas Ashley, upon presentation by Sir John Marny. (Bishop Vesey's Reg. fol. 18.)

Edmund Bedyngfyld(e)/Benyfeld

Under the entry for John Bere, in the List of Rectors of Endellion, reference was made (in 1537) to Edmund Bedyngfyld as Prebend of Marny's. We shall see that Ralph Hartopp succeeded him because of the vacancy caused by his "deprivation".

Edmund Benyfeld is mentioned in the Chantry Certificates 9/18, 15/91 and 10/19 apropos "An Acte for the Dissolution of Colleges, Chantries, and Free Chappells at the King's Majesties Pleasure". (The Chantries Act of 1545, 37 Hen.VIII c.4.) We have already considered this Act in the essay on St Endelienta's Foundation.

Reference to Chantry Certificate 9/18 must be made here because it reminds us that William Cavell was Prebend of Trehaverock, Edmund Benyfeld of Marny's and John Parry of Bodmin Prebends. At the same time we must recall that all three received pensions of £5 in connection with the pensions paid to dispossessed religious. (See the Roll of Fees paid to members of Suppressed Chantries and Religious Houses out of the Exchequer: 2nd & 3rd Philip & Mary. B.M. Add.Mss. 8102.)

Ralph Hartopp, Clerk **17th February 1558**

He was admitted "to a Canonry, or portion, in the Church of St Endellion", vacant by the deprivation of Edmond Bedyngfield, upon presentation by Lord Thomas Howard Viscount Bindon. (Bishop Turbeville's Reg. fol. 45.)

Sir Richard Lillington, Clerk **3rd January 1577**

He was admitted to the Prebend of "St Ellens vulgarly called Marnys" upon presentation by Lord Thomas Howard of Bindon. (Bishop Alley's Reg. fol. 41.) We do not know the cause of the vacancy which he filled.

William Hayte, M.A. **9th September 1586**

He was instituted by Bishop John Woolton, filling the vacancy caused by the death of Sir Richard Lillington, upon presentation by Henry Howard Viscount Bindon.

Thomas Barrett **1589**

He was admitted to "the Prebend of Marneis, alias St Ellens". (Bishop's Certs. of Inst., Aug.Off.)

Christopher Strange **5th April 1603**

He was instituted on the resignation of Thomas Barrett upon presentation by Richard Newman by grant of Thomas Harries, Sergeant at Law.

John Carter **No date**

His tenure and death are mentioned below.

Walter Snell, Clerk **4th July 1663**

Admitted to the prebend, vacant by the death of John Carter, upon presentation by John Lord Robartes Baron of Truro. (Bishop Gauden's Reg. fol. 61.)

Philip Dinham, B.A. **4th April 1678**

Admitted to the prebend, vacant by the death of Walter Snell, upon presentation by John Lord Robartes. (Bishop Lamplugh's Reg. fol. 86.) His father was John Dinham of St Kew. He matriculated at Exeter College, Oxford in 1642. He had been appointed Rector of Blisland (1660) where he was buried on 30th January 1708–9. (Parish Reg. Blisland.)

Jonathan Phillibrowe, M.A. **28th October 1686**

Admitted to the prebend, vacant by the resignation of Philip Dinham, upon presentation by Charles Bodville, Earl of Radnor. (Bishop Lamplugh's Reg. fol. 67.) He matriculated at Queen's College, Cambridge, B.A. 1680, M.A. 1684.

John Baker, Clerk **7th January 1695**

Admitted to the prebend, vacant by the resignation of Jonathan Phillipbrowe, upon presentation by Charles Bodville, Earl of Radnor. (Bishop's Reg. New Series Vol.IV fol. 13.)

William Pennington, B.A. **20th October 1716**

Admitted to the prebend, vacant by the death of John Baker, upon presentation by Charles Bodville, Earl of Radnor. (Bishop's Reg. New Series Vol.V fol. 96.) He was son of Christopher Pennington of Bodmin. He matriculated at Exeter College, Oxford, B.A. 1701.

Daniel Debat, M.A. **19th October 1738**

Admitted to the prebend, vacant by the death of William Pennington, upon presentation by Henry Roberts(Robartes), Earl of Radnor. (Bishop's Reg. New Series Vol.VII fol. 48.) He was son of James Debat of London. He matriculated at Gloucester Hall, Oxford, B.A. 1706, M.A. 1710.

Thomas Nevil, Clerk **2nd October 1765**

Admitted to the prebend, vacant by the death of Daniel Debat, upon presentation by George Hunt of Lanhydrock. (Bishop's Reg. New Series Vol.II fol. 10.)

John Cole, B.A. **7th March 1770**

Admitted to the prebend, vacant by the death of Thomas Nevil, upon presentation by George Hunt. (Bishop's Reg. New Series Vol.II fol. 50.) He was son of Francis Cole of Lanivet. He matriculated at Exeter College, Oxford, B.A. 1726.

John Fisher, B.A. **12th May 1773**

Admitted to the prebend, vacant by the death of John Cole, upon presentation by George Hunt. (Bishop's Reg. New Series Vol.II fol. 83.) He was Master of the Grammar School, Bodmin.

John Fisher, B.A. **13th March 1777**

Admitted to the prebend, vacant by the death of John Fisher, upon presentation by George Hunt. (Bishop's Reg. New Series Vol.IX fol. 128.) He was son of John Fisher of Bodmin, Clerk. He matriculated at Exeter College, Oxford, B.A. 1763.

William Flamank, M.A. **15th September 1777**

Admitted to the prebend, vacant by the resignation of John Fisher, upon presentation by George Hunt. (Bishop's Reg. New Series Vol.IX fol. 135.)

Joseph Fayrer, M.A. **27th December 1817**

Admitted to the prebend, vacant by the death of William Flamank, upon presentation by the Hon. Anna Maria Agar of Lanhydrock, widow. (Bishop's Reg. New Series Vol.XI fol. 98.) He matriculated at Clare College, Cambridge, B.A. 1809, M.A. 1817. He was Vicar of Lanhydrock and afterwards (1821) of St Teath.

Nicholas Kendall, M.A. **4th October 1838**

Admitted to the prebend, vacant by the death of Joseph Fayrer, upon presentation by the Hon. Anna Maria Agar. (BRNS Vol.XII fol. 135.) He was Vicar of Lanhydrock (1831).

Charles Crylls, B.A. **22nd October 1844**

Instituted to the prebend, vacant by the death of Nicholas Kendall, upon presentation by the Hon. Anna Maria Agar. (BRNS Vol.XIII fol. 19.) He matriculated at Trinity College, Cambridge, B.A. 1833. He was Vicar of Lanhydrock (22nd October 1844).

Bodmin Prebend

Prebend	*Date*	*Patron*	*Bishop's Register*
Henry de Monketon	1294	See below[2]	
William de Monketon	1314		
Master John de Bos	1342	Prior and Convent of Bodmin	
William de Doune[3]			
Master Symon Withiell	1361 or 1373		
Noel (alias Christmas) **Karnnellow**	30th Oct. 1376	–do–	Brentingham Vol.III fol.43
Master William Tregoys			
Robert Vaggescombe (he had been Canon and Prebendary of the Collegiate Church of Glasney and exchanged with William Tregoys)	30th July 1380	–do–	ibid. fol.65

[2] It is highly probable that the Prior and Convent of Bodmin held the patronage of this prebend from the beginning and that the possibility of the Monketon family having held it originally is doubtful. It was in existence in 1294 (Taxation of the Bishops of Lincoln and Winchester) when Henry de Monketon was presumably presented by the Priory. Nevertheless, when he was succeeded by William de Monketon in 1314, Sir Richard de St Margaret (who had been appointed a portioner in 1312 by the Bishop by reason of the default of the Priory) opposed presentation by the Priory. A long drawn out litigation involving two commissions (April 1314 and August 1324) ordered by the Bishop (Walter de Stapeldon's Reg. folios 84 & 163) resulted in findings against Sir Richard and for William de Monketon. This somewhat complicated affair may well have been a domestic matter in which there was a clash of personalities.

[3] William de Doune provides us with an interesting example of pluralism. He was Bishop Grandisson's clerk and notary when he was appointed to this prebend. The Bishop petitioned the Pope for a dispensation for him to receive further benefices in addition to that of Prebend of Bodmin to which he was appointed in 1342. In 1343 the Bishop petitioned the Pope that William be allowed to hold three benefices without ordination to the Priesthood and the obligation to reside. In 1354 William had accumulated the position of Official of the Dioceses of Lincoln and Worcester, Archdeacon of Leicester, Rector of Quainton in addition to his Prebend of Bodmin. It is small wonder that, in that year, he was himself petitioning for the confirmation of his latest appointment as Archdeacon. Such pluralism and consequent absenteeism reflects upon the Priory's concern for the spiritual welfare of the parishioners of Endellion.

Master Hugh de Hickelyng	19th June 1382	–do–	ibid. fol.72
John Halle			
Master Richard Bruton (formerly Rector of Burghwardescote, he exchanged with John Halle)	16th Jan. 1391	–do–	ibid. fol.120
John Arundell	27th Dec. 1417	–do–	Stafford fol.189
Robert King (Chaplain)	15th April 1421	–do–	Lacey Vol.II fol.49
Robert Symon	13th March 1440	–do–	ibid. fol.193
Thomas Nayler (Chaplain)	18th Nov. 1456	–do–	Nevill folios 3 & 86
Nicholas Milionek	6th May 1472	–do–	Bothe fol.21
John Baby			
James Hetton	20th Dec. 1523	–do–	Veysey, fol.107
Thomas Vivian (possibly Vyvyan, he was Prior of Bodmin and Bishop of Megara)	20th Jan. 1524	John Chamond by grant of Bodmin Priory	ibid. fol.17
Thomas Brerwode, D.D. (see under John Bere, Rector of St Endellion)	1st July 1533	William Vyvyan by Grant of Bodmin P.	Veysey fol.67
John Par(RY) (see Edmund Benyfeld, Marny's)	3rd Oct. 1542	See below[4]	ibid. fol.108
Giles Boteler	10th Aug. 1564		
William Boteler (Lay Scholar)	6th April 1587	John Botelier	Babington fol.31
Peter Shepherd	24th July 1596	Balthazar Botelier	ibid. fol.61
John Pyne	25th July 1611		Carey fol.95
Philip Boteler	26th May 1616		ibid. fol.106
John Orchard, M.A. (Gloucester Hall Oxon.)	22nd Oct. 1661	William Leigh	Gauden fol.21
Henry Taylor	1st June 1675	John Basset	Lamplugh fol.38
John Ackland, M.A.	5th June 1682		BRNS Vol.III fol.26

[4] John Par(ry) and Simon Repyngton by grant of Sir John Chamond who received the same from John Symonds, late Prior of Bodmin. A double devolution indeed.

Tobias Langdon	10th Aug. 1690	Francis Basset	BRNS fol.100
Gilbert Langdon (Exeter College, Oxon.)	24th July 1712	John Belfield	ibid. Vol.V fol.62
Thomas Morrison (New College, Oxon.)	5th May 1736	John Basset	ibid. Vol.VI fol.156
William Cooke	5th Jan. 1779	Francis Basset	ibid. Vol.IX fol.152
George Burgess, B.A.	2nd Jan. 1793		ibid. Vol.X fol.83
John Boyce	8th Aug. 1797		ibid. fol.120
John Comyns (Queen's College, Oxon.)	27th Sept. 1850	Thomas Comins	ibid. Vol.XIII fol.71

TREHAVEROCK PREBEND

Prebend	*Date*	*Patron*	*Bishop's Register*
John Bloyou (Sub-Deacon)	1266	Robert Modret	Bronescombe fol.16
John Modret (Sub-Deacon)	1269	Robert Modret	ibid.
Richard de St Margaret	1296		
John Bray			
Matthew Bodrygy (Canon and Prebendary of the Collegiate Church of St Thomas, Glasney by exchange with John Bray)	6th Oct. 1392	William Bray	Brentingham fol.136
Henry Wyket	3rd June 1400	Sir John Arundel (by grant Elizabeth with W. Bray)	Stafford fol.46
John Cavel	18th Dec. 1428	Nicholas Cavell	Lacy, Vol.II fol.88
Richard Tregoos	21st Dec. 1461	Peter Tregoos	Nevill fol.18

William Cavell (See John Bere, Rector and Edmund Benyfeld Prebendary of Marny's)	*c.* 1537		
John Goldsmith	8th April 1591	John Cavell	Babington fol.47
Henry Hazill	21st July 1605	William Cavell	Carey fol.82
Ralph Hadon	6th May 1618	William Cavell	Carey fol.110
Christopher Strong	21st July 1628	The King (by reason of simony)	Hall fol.4
John Orchard			
John Wills (on death of John Orchard)	28th May 1675	John Vivian	Sparrow fol.37
John Richardson (Exeter College, Oxon., B.A.1685, M.A.1688)	16th June 1708	William Harper	New Series Vol.V fol.4
Jonathan Dagge, M.A. (also Rector; see under Rectors for details of him)	12th Feb. 1717	John Gray, Richardson Gray and Catherine Gray	ibid. fol.113; see also Vol.IV fol.14
John Dagge, M.A. (also Rector; see under Rectors for details of him)	31st Dec. 1733	John Gray	ibid. Vol.VI fol.96
Mydhope Wallis (also Rector; see under Rectors for details of him)	7th April 1753	Catherine Dagge, w. John Dagge	ibid. Vol.VIII fol.20
Thomas Poulton	13th Dec. 1754	Catherine Dagge	New Series fol.36
John Thome/Thomas (Exeter College, Oxon., matric. 1709/10?)	26th March 1784	William Gray	ibid. Vol.X fol.2
John Kempe (also Vicar of Fowey 9th Oct. 1818)	3rd June 1818	Richardson Gray	ibid. Vol.XI fol.103

Prelude to the Rehabilitation

Charles James Blomfield (Bishop of London from 1828 to 1856) was of the opinion that the Ecclesiastical Commission, brought into being by Sir Robert Peel, saved the Church of England. It certainly saved the Collegiate Church of St Endelienta from suppression and made possible its rehabilitation. Why was St Endellion, for the second time, spared? The Dean and Chapter Act of 1840, which legalized some of the recommendations of the commission, resulted in the suppression of some 360 non-resident prebends. Somehow, in spite of the diligence and efficiency of the commission, St Endellion was overlooked. Its remoteness was not the reason for there were equally remote foundations which were suppressed. It is more likely that it was providentially saved for a purpose.

The missionary work inaugurated by St Endelienta and continued by that small colony of priests united in a ministry "perhaps better described as something part-way between a clergy-house and a religious order" and, after the Norman Conquest, transformed into a Collegiate foundation during the existence of which that work, even if to a varying degree of faithfulness and zeal, was maintained was in evidence, not least, during the nineteenth century. In July 1882 the late Canon Carter planned an itinerary mission which embraced the parishes of St Endellion, St Minver and St Kew. The reconstitution of Cornwall as a diocese with its see at Truro in 1877 and its succession of pastoral and missionary minded bishops has brought new spiritual life into the Cornish Peninsular and revived the missionary work of those Celtic Christians who lived in what has aptly been called the Age of the Saints. Such a foundation as that of St Endelienta is one of the links with that glorious past. Its rehabilitation has ensured its survival, confirmed for posterity by a Pastoral Scheme made by Order in Council in 1973.

From the Rehabilitation Onwards

The *Truro Diocesan Gazette* for June 1929 informs us, *inter alia*, in its account of the rehabilitation of "Our Prebendal Church" that: "This great thing over the assembled company went to luncheon. Subsequently, so rumour hath it, the chapter of Endellion met in conclave for the first recorded time, while the bishop ruminated outside on the prebendal lawns."

There was indeed a Chapter Meeting at 2 p.m. on 2nd May 1929 during which the Bishop may well have taken a discreet post-prandial perambulation but the Minutes Book of the Chapter informs us that the Chapter had met, "probably for the first time for several centuries", in the previous year on 9th May 1928.

This meeting, over which Bishop Walter Frere presided, was of considerable historical importance and undoubtedly paved the way for the rehabilitation which was to take place in the following year. Sad to relate, the Rector of St Endellion was absent through illness but the three other Prebendaries were present. The latter resolved to: "pray the Lord Bishop to grant the Chapter such statutes as would be conducive to the welfare and usefulness of the Society".

The Minutes further record that: "the Rector [although *in absentia*] and Prebendaries having agreed as to the Statutes, and perhaps to a short office to be said daily, a Petition should be presented to the Lord Bishop praying that Statutes and a corporate life should be given to the Chapter."

These requests were, of course, readily granted and the Minutes of that meeting held at 2 p.m. on 2nd May 1929 record that at 11 a.m. the Holy Eucharist was celebrated by the Rector in the presence of the Bishop at the end of which "the Bishop re-constituted the prebendal body, reading the ordinatio, ordaining statutes and receiving the homage of the Prebendaries". At this meeting, too, various unspecified proposals were made for future Chapter Meetings.

The Chapter got off to a good start. It met on 30th April 1930 when it could report that the Statutes had been kept during the past year. On 29th April 1931, however, it failed to meet because of the absence of three Prebendaries and there is a pathetic little note in the Minutes Book which tells us that: "The Rector said the Devotion by himself in Choir."

Thereafter the Chapter met at least annually and sometimes more frequently–twice in 1932, 1948, 1954, 1962, 1973 and 1974; three times in 1950 and 1953; even four times in 1955 and 1956 for example. There were occasions when one or two Prebendaries absented themselves from Chapter Meetings because of age, ill health or distance. At the meeting held on 3rd May 1933 one of the absentees "mistook the day".

Such understandable absenteeism, not unknown among the Clergy at large as far as Chapter Meetings are concerned, did not impede the smooth running of prebendal and parochial affairs. The Rector was always around and one might say that just as St Endellion has been fortunate in its Prebendaries it has been particularly fortunate in its Rectors.

Over the years the Prebendaries observed the Statutes though there is an interesting rider, viz. "so far as they were able to do so", in the Minutes of the Chapter Meeting held on 29th April 1941. They were also diligent in the saying of the Devotion but human and honest about this obligation. The Minutes of the Chapter Meeting held on 21st July 1948 record that two Prebendaries "had found it difficult to avoid occasional forgetfulness, a fact which bears out past general experience that a weekly obligation is hard to remember and fulfil unless tied mechanically to a set time or unvarying occasion".

Chapter Business certainly covered a wide spectrum ranging from the restoration of the Collegiate Church to the provision of stalls for the Prebendaries in the Mother Church of the Diocese, from the grant of Arms to the Prebendal Chapter from the Earl Marshall to the omission of mention of the Collegiate Foundation in Crockford's *Clerical Directory* and from the great matter of the Littleham advowson to prebendal glebe and property.

From the episcopate of Bishop Walter Frere to that of Bishop Graham Leonard the Chapter was enjoyed a cordial relationship with its Diocesan Bishop who in addition to being its Father in God has also now become Patron of all four Prebendaries. Lay patronage may well have saved the foundation from suppression; episcopal patronage will ensure its continued survival.

The only possible episcopal fly in the ointment was perhaps the late Bishop J.W. Hunkin who, with the best of intentions, commented on pre-Reformation sinecures when he instituted a prebendary in 1949. His sermon, on that occasion, evoked a gentle rebuke from the then Rector of St Ervan.

If any damage was unintentionally done by Bishop Hunkin it was rectified by his successors in office and not least by Bishop Graham Leonard who, following in the footsteps of Bishop Walter Frere, addressed the four Prebendaries of St Endellion on 4th May 1974 at a Chapter Meeting held after he had celebrated and preached at a Solemn Eucharist.

In this, he parted company from his predecessor in that he pontificated and preached at the Solemn Eucharist and, rather than ruminate on the prebendal lawns, he attended the Chapter Meeting on the Feast of Title. Characteristically he advocated that a close relationship between the Prebendaries might well be effected by frequent Eucharistic worship together. The Chapter responded by agreeing to hold a quarterly Chapter Meeting in rotation at each other's places of residence preceded by a Eucharist.

The corporate life of the Chapter has become linked with that of the Parish of St Endellion which, under its recent Parish Priest and Rector has catered not only for regular Churchgoers but also for an ever widening circle of music lovers by the means of the St Endellion Music Festivals. These draw people to the Shrine of St Endelienta and it is to be hoped that in the enjoyment of music in such a sacred spot those who attend them may become aware of an atmosphere of sanctity which has to do with Eternal Life.

Nicholas Roscarrock's Life of St Endelienta

Of St Endelienta

Apr. 29. Sainct Endelient was as I am informed out of the life of her brother St Nectan, the daughter of the often named St Brechanus by his wife Gladuse. She lived in a place in Cornwall called Trenteny, where I remember there stoode a Chappell dedicated (as I take it) to her which at this daye is decayed, and the place in which it stoode is yet called the Chappele Cloose, and lyeth on the south-west of the Parrish Church, which at this present is of her called St Endelient, where shee lived a verie Austere Course of life. That with the Milke of a Cowe onelye which Cowe the lord of Trenteny kild as she strayed into his grounds; and as olde people speaking by Tradition, doe report she had a great man to her Godfather, which they also saye was King Arthure, whoe toke the killing of the Cowe in such sort, as he killed or caused the Man to be slaine, whom she miraculously revived. And when she perceived the daye of her death drawe nye, she intreated her friends after her death, to laye her dead bodye on a sled and to burie her there where certaine young Scots Bullocks or Calves of a yere olde should of their owne accord drawe her, which being done, they brought her to a place, which at that tyme was a Myrye waste grounde, and a great quagmire on the topp of an hill, where in time after there was a Church builded on her and dedicated to her, bearing her name, which since proved a fyne firme and fruitfull part of grounde, where her ffeast was accustomed to be yerely remembered the 29 of Aprill, and I have heard it credablye reported, that the Chappell in Lundy, was likewise dedicated unto her and bare her name; yet my good friend Mr Camden saith the Chappell was dedicated unto St Heline; but under correction, except hee have no better warrant, than bare Coniecture, I still holde the former report more likely partelye because her brother St

Nectan had a Church dedicated at Harty pointe over against it, but 14 miles from it; next being not farr from St Endelian in Cornwall, and uppon the same sea Coast, by reason whereof it is not improbable that shee did alsoe sometimes live in that Island for manie of St Brechanns Children plantted themselves neere on another. As this St Endelient, St Memfrey or St Menefred St Maben, St Tuddy etc. And yet I doe not as much as finde her Named, in twoe severall Pedegrees, except they gave her som other name. Reed St Brechanus, and St Nectan, perhapps the booke of landaff calleth her Belian the 21 daughter of St Bechanus.

The Collector writeth to and of his Patronesse as followeth:–

Sweit Sainct Endelienta virgin pure
   Daughter of Prince and Sainct, yea Sister deare;
   Of manie Sts. which stowtlie didst indure
   Conflictes in Worlde with Sinners living here
Voucsaife sweit Sainct, my Patronesse to bee
To praye for him whoe humblye prayes to thee.

To thee which being borne of Royall Blood
   Having the world as twere at thy owne will,
   Leftes all to follow God true Soveraigne Good
   Who onelye able was thy Sowle to fill
Daunting the worlde, the flesh, the feind and Sin,
For liffe well led, an endless life to win.

ffor which a Sainct thow worthirlie art Crownd
   In heaven above with everlasting bliss
   and here on earth belowe likewise renownd
   Where to thy name a Church erected is
Even there where thowe they Life didst lead and leave
And where I wretch true life did first receive.

ffor in that church a Christian I became
   And of Christes Church a Member first to bee
   And also was Confirmed in the same
   for which I thank my god and praye to thee
This work to further in thy Church begun
with prayer that I my raise may rightly Run.

To emitate in part thy vertues rare
  Thy faith, Hope, Charitie, thy humble mynde
  Thy Chastness, meekness, and thy dyet spare
  And that which in this Worlde is hard to finde
The love which thow to enemye didst showe
Reviving him who sought thy overthrowe.

Unto the three and one priae thow for this
  And all thy fellow Saintes with mee request
  That I maye shun to Sin and doe amiss
  Bewaile sins past and followe Gods behest
Graunt me this Grace good God whose might is moste
Thrice Blessed ffather, Soun, and Holi Ghoste.

There were twoe Wells which bare her Name in the forementioned Parish, the one somewhat more distant from the Church then the other, which hathe bene as it seams found out of late, for more conveniencie to serve the Church; but that which is more remote, is said to be frequented by her in her life time. Her Tombe was defaced in King Henrie the 8 time and afterwardes placed uppon one Mr Batten in Chandutes Ile, being the South Aile of her Church, where it standeth at this present, and seameth to have bene verie Auncient. The Table where of is of Pollished stone like black Marble.
Reed St Eudeline.

Of St Eudeline or Endeline Virgin

ffabrua 18. ffather Whitford fabruarie the 18, in his Additions to the Englishe translated Martriloge maketh mention of a Virgin named Eudeline or Endeline, whose ffeast was observed in England on that daye, but I cannot learne whoe she should be; unless it were St Endelaine, or St Endelient. But her ffeast is kept in the Parrish which beareth her name in Cornwalle the 29th of Aprill unless she had twoe ffeasts.

List of Prebends since the Mid-nineteenth Century

Rectors

Reginald Heber Treffry	1880
Fortuno Pietro Luigi Josa	1917
Richard Tolson Schlesinger	1923
Arthur William Gerald Murphy	1932
William Henry Prior	1956
Arthur Charles Williams	1965
Walter Prest	1970

Marny's

John James Glencross Every	1876
Thomas Henry Wood	1915
Herbert Alldridge Abbott	1946
Gordon Lawes	1959
Edwin George John Stark	1981

Bodmin or King's

Arthur Crawfurth Basset	1870
Francis Edward Carter	1880
Arthur Lindsay Palmes	1885
Wilfrid Ryan Johnson	1946
Arthur Gerald Sayer	1954
Howard Miles Brown	1973

Trehaverock

Frederick Bell	1863
Reginald Heber Treffry	1890
Francis Davis Moat	1928
Harnett Ellisson Jennings	1937
William James Margetson	1939
Guy Wittenoon Hockley	1946

Ernest Scott	1947
Arthur Longden	1949
William John Peter Boyd	1973

Ordinatio

WALTER, by Divine permission, Bishop of Truro, to all whom it may concern, whether within the Diocese of Truro or elsewhere, greeting.

It is of common knowedge that the Church of Saint Endelienta, commonly called Saint Endellion, has been from time immemorial equipped with four Prebendaries, each holding an independent Prebend; moreover one of them has from very early times served the cure of the Church, while the others have been non-resident and have held no cure of souls therein. This Prebendal Foundation escaped the suppression which overcame the greater part of such churches in the middle of the 16th century; and again it escaped the suppression which overtook other Collegiate or Prebendal Churches in the 19th century; consequently it still survives to-day. The advowson of the Rectory and Prebend with cure of souls has recently passed by arrangement from the Crown to ourselves and our successors. The other three Prebends are now held thus: one is in the hands of the Right Honourable Viscount Clifden, that is to say, the Prebend of Marny, and the other two, the Prebend of Bodmin or Kings and the Prebend of Trehaverock, are in the patronage of Athelstan Riley, Esquire.

A petition has been presented to us by the holders of the several Prebends begging us to recognize them as forming an ecclesiastical and prebendal body and to ordain Statutes for their common observance.

WE, therefore, being willing to grant the petition, and having received the assent of the two patrons other than ourselves, do hereby recognize the said Church of Saint Endelienta as a Prebendal Church, and the four Prebendaries as forming an ecclesiastical body whereof the Rector has the cure of souls. And we do by these presents appoint the Statutes annexed hereto to be the Statutes of the said Prebendal Body. Moreover we do declare, on behalf of ourselves and of our successors, that in future appointments to the Rectorial

Prebend regard shall be had to the observance of these Statutes by the person so to be appointed; and we exhort the patrons of the other Prebends to do the like. So this Prebendal Church which has almost by a miracle escaped destruction, shall hereafter be continued in its ancient form, and may serve for the Glory of God, for the good of the Parish, and for the common life and worship of the Prebendaries.

And we do declare, as far as in us lies, that those in the future shall be appointed to the Prebends, on their declaration thay they will observe faithfully the Statutes aforesaid, shall enjoy the full benefits of the said Prebendal Body, and we authorize them to wear the habit assigned to the Prebendaries, and to be taken and reputed in all things throughout our Diocese as Prebendaries of the Prebendal Church of Saint Endelienta aforesaid; the rights and privileges of our Cathedral Church at Truro being in all respects saved.

And that this our ordinance may have the greater effect we have obtained the assent thereto of the Residentiary Chapter of the Cathedral Church at Truro, and of the Greater Chapter of the same.

Statutes of the Prebendal Church of St Endelienta

1. The Rector and other Prebendaries of the Church of Saint Endelienta in the Diocese of Truro, when they have been duly instituted, inducted and installed, and after giving their adhesion to the Statutes following, shall be taken and reputed as full Members of the Prebendal Body; being bound together by spiritual ties only as follows;
2. They shall pray daily for one another, and especially for the Rector in his cure of souls, for the Church and the Parish, using weekly the common form hereto annexed[1] in discharge of this their duty of prayer.
3. Once at least in the year each of them shall celebrate the Holy Mysteries with special intention for the Prebendal Body.
4. Each Prebendary who has no cure of souls in the Parish of Saint Endelienta shall, unless reasonably hindered, visit the church at least once in the year and do service in the said church; habited in the prescribed dress, namely, his cassock and surplice, together with the almuce assigned by the Bishop as proper to the foundation and its full members.
5. On the 29th Day of April in each year, being the Feast of the Patroness, or on some day in the Octave of the same, Holy Communion shall be celebrated in the Prebendal Church, with the Collects, Epistle, and Gospel hereafter provided; and all the Prebendaries shall make it their aim to be present thereat, and join in common worship.

   The Rector, after consultation with his brethren, shall fix the day of this annual service, and notify it to the rest.
6. Every non-resident Prebendary shall be ready, if opportunity arises, to help the Rector in his parochial charge, or to supply his place, if able and invited to do so, when he is lawfully absent.
7. The Rector shall report yearly to the Bishop, as Visitor of the

Prebendal Body, on the observance of these Statutes within the week following the annual service.

8. Declaration to be made on admission to a Prebend:

   "I.........................do declare that I assent to the Statutes of the Prebendal Church of Saint Endelienta, and that I will faithfully observe and obey them."

The Eucharist for St Endelienta's Feast-day (29th April)

Introit The ungodly laid wait for me to destroy me, but I will consider Thy testimonies, O Lord: I see that all things come to an end, but Thy commandments are exceeding broad.
Ps. Blessed are those that are undefiled in the way: and walk in the law of the Lord. Glory. The ungodly.

Collect O ALMIGHTY and everlasting God, who art the author of all virtue, and lover of Virginity: Grant, we beseech Thee, that like as the Blessed Endelienta, by virtuous life and singleness of heart, was found well pleasing unto Thee, so we, profiting by her prayer and her example, may now and ever find favour in Thy sight. Through. .

Epistle II Corinthians 10:17–11:2.

Gradual. THOU has loved righteousness and hated iniquity, Wherefore God, even thy God, hath anointed thee with the oil of gladness. Alleluia, full of grace are thy lips: because God hath blessed thee for ever. Alleluia.

Gospel St Matthew, 25:1–13. JESUS spake this parable to His disciples: The Kingdom...wherein the Son of Man cometh.

Offertory FULL of grace are thy lips because God hath blessed thee for ever.

Secret. AS we offer Thee, O Lord, our prayers and gifts, rejoicing in honour of Saint Endelienta, Thy Virgin: Grant, we beseech Thee, that we may both fitly perform this service, and obtain the benefit of Thy everlasting mercy, Through....

Post Communion LET the mysteries we have received be profitable to us, we beseech Thee, O Lord: And at the intercession of Thy blessed Virgin Endelienta, both set us free from our sins, and raise us up to the protection of Thy favour and mercy. Through....

A Devotion for the Weekly Use of the Prebendaries

Ant. Come, thou Bride of Christ: receive the crown, which the Lord hath prepared for thee for ever. (Alleluia.)
V. Full of grace are thy lips. (Alleluia.)
R. Because God hath blessed thee for ever. (Alleluia.)

Let us pray.

ALMIGHTY and everlasting god, who art the Author of all virtues, and Lover of Virginity: Grant, we beseech Thee, that like as the Blessed Endelienta, by virtuous life and singleness of heart, was found well-pleasing unto Thee, so we, profiting by her prayer and her example, may now and ever find favour in Thy sight. Through....

O Lord God of Hosts, Who didst give grace to Thy servant Endelienta to lay aside the fear of men, and to live a devoted life in the confession of Thy name: Grant that all who bear office in Thy Church may think lightly of earthly place and honour; and seek rather to please the Captain of our salvation, Who hath chosen them to be His soldiers; to whom with Thee and the Holy Ghost be honour and praise from all the armies of the Saints now and for evermore. Amen.

GRANT, O Lord God, that as we bless Thy Holy Name for the sweet fragrance of Saint Endelienta's holy life: So we, the Rector and Prebendaries of Saint Endelienta, may ever remember her faith, her purity and her devotion to Thy service; and may strive, by self denial and forgiveness of injuries, to follow her example. Through....

V. Let us bless the Lord.
R. Thanks be to God.

May the souls of the faithful, through the mercy of God, rest in peace. Amen.

Bibliography

BETJEMAN, JOHN (Ed.) *Collins Guide to English Parish Churches.* Collins, 1958.

BOWEN, E.G. *Saints, Seaways and Settlements in the Celtic Lands.* Cardiff: University of Wales Press, 1977.

COOK, G.H. *English Collegiate Churches.* London: Phoenix House Ltd, 1959.

COX, J. CHARLES *County Churches–Cornwall.* George Allen & Co. Ltd., 1912.

DOBLE, GILBERT H. *S. Nectan, S.Keyne and the Children of Brychan in Cornwall* (Cornish Saints Series No.25). Exeter: Sydney Lee Ltd. 1930.

DOBLE, GILBERT H. *The Life of Saint Nectan* (Cornish Saints Series No.48). Bideford: Polypress Ltd, 1964.

DONALDSON, A.B. *The Bishopric of Truro* (1877–1902). Rivington,s 1902.

FARMER, DAVID HUGH *The Oxford Dictionary of Saints* Oxford: Clarendon Press, 1978.

GUEST, JOHN *The Best of Betjeman.* Penguin Books in association with John Murray, 1978.

LACH-SZYRMA, W.S. *A Church History of Cornwall and of the Diocese of Truro.* London: Elliot Stock, Plymouth: Church in the West. Truro: Netherton and Worth (N.D.).

PEARCE, SUSAN M. *The Kingdom of Dumnonia* (A.D. 350–1150) Padstow: Lodenek Press, 1978.

PHILLIPS, C.S. *et al.* *Walter Howard Frere, A Memoir.* Faber and Faber, 1947.

PEVSNER, NIKOLAUS *The Buildings of England: Cornwall,* 2nd Edition, revised by Enid Radcliffe, Penguin Books, 1970.

SNELL, LAWRENCE S. *The Suppression of the Religious Foundations of Devon and Cornwall.* Wordens of Cornwall Ltd, 1967.

SNELL, LAWRENCE S. *Documents towards a History of the Reformation in Cornwall:* No. 1. *The Chantry Certificates for Cornwall* No. 2. *The Edwardian inventories of Church Goods for Cornwall.* Exeter: printed by James Townsend & Sons Ltd (N.D.).

TAYLOR, THOMAS *The Celtic Christianity of Cornwall.* Longmans, Green & Co., 1916.

TAYLOR, THOMAS *St Endellion Prebendal Church: Its Constitution and History.* Truro: Oscar Blackford, 1929.

TURNER, JAMES *The Stone Peninsular.* London: William Kimber, 1975.

Printed Original Sources

Registers of the Bishops of Exeter edited by F.C. Hingeston-Randolph and published by George Bell:

Walter Bronescombe (1257–80)
Peter Quivil (1280–91) together with Records of Thomas de Bytton (1292–1307) and the Taxation of Pope Nicholas IV (1291):
Diocese of Exeter: S. Endellion p. 471 (1889)
Walter de Stapeldon (1307–26) (1892)
John de Grandisson (1327–69) 3p (1894–9)
Thomas de Brantyngham (1370–94) 2p (1901–6)
Edmund Stafford (1395–1419) (1886)
Edited by G.R. DUNSTAN and published by The Devon & Cornwall Record Society (1972):
Edmund Lacey (1420–1455).